RED GOLDFISH

MOTIVATING SALES AND LOYALTY THROUGH SHARED PASSION AND PURPOSE

STAN PHELPS

&

GRAEME NEWELL

Published by 9 INCH

Copy Editing by Lee Heinrich of Write Way Publishing Company LLC

ISBN: 978-0-9849838-7-2

1. Purpose 2. Leadership 3. Culture 4. Organizational Effectiveness

First Printing: 2017

Printed in the United States of America

Red Goldfish is available for bulk orders. For further details and special pricing, please e-mail stan@purplegoldfish.com.

This book is dedicated to my late brother John Phelps, Jr.
His passion was contagious, his laugh was infectious,
and his spirit was courageous. He lives on in our hearts.

—Stan Phelps

This book is dedicated to Larry Rickel.
Thank you for showing me how an authentic business mission
can uplift an entire community

—Graeme Newell

ACKNOWLEDGEMENTS

We'd like to thank everyone who inspired us, supported us, or provided feedback for this book:

Jennifer Phelps, Annette Newell, Cory Richardson, Christopher Warren, Harrison Wyatt, Greg Derkowski, Larry Rickel, Theodemae Maliza, David Howitt, Fred Wills, Chris Malone, John Mackey, Lisa Earle McLoud Simon Sinek, John Kotter, James Heskett, Ted Levitt, Evan Carroll, Raj Sisodia, Dave Rendall, S. Chris Edmonds, Mark Levy, Yvon Chouinard, Vineet Nayar, Tony Hsieh, Susan T. Fiske, Milton Friedman, Chip Conley, Joey Reiman, Dan Pontefract, Aaron Hurst, Dan Pink, Thomas Friedman, Mark Twain, Lou Gerstner, Ricardo Semler, Jeff Bezos, Sam Walton, Jack Welch, Ted Coiné, Rebecca Smith, Simon Mainwaring, Bono, Bobby Shriver, Abraham Maslow, Joseph Campbell, Mark Twain, Richard Branson, Ed Freeman, Benjamin Disraeli, Peter Drucker, Shubro Sen, Jeff Klein, Lee Heinrich, Kevin Snyder, Jay Baer, John Andrews, Ted Rubin, Roy M. Spence Jr., Michelle Newell, Christy Fritz, Mark Lange, Lawrence McKay, Lauren Ridgley, Linda Peach, Karl Sakas, Chuck Gallagher, Lucinda Newell, Erik Larson, Dyvontrae Johnson, Janice Sweeter, Café Carolina, and The Frontier at RTP

CONTENTS

FOREWORD

BY DAVID HOWITT

"The dogmas of the quiet past are
inadequate to the stormy present."

- Abraham Lincoln

The most important word for any leader today is **And**. No longer is it enough to simply run a profitable business. Employees and consumers demand more. We instinctively want to support companies with strong purposes that bring value into the world. We appreciate those who care deeply for the well being of their staff and consumers and who are mindful about their business practices.

As CEO of the Meriwether Group, a company that provides strategic vision to entrepreneurs in a time renowned for its hunger for authenticity, I've found that my clients share one main goal: they are all striving to create meaningful and profitable brands. My own journey as an entrepreneur, outlined in my book *Heed Your Call*, taught me that to be a truly successful business, we must embrace the power of And.

A RELATIONSHIP WITH AND

In order to contextualize the **And** model, we first need to understand the **Tyranny of Or**. As youth, our superiors intentionally and unintentionally program us to adopt Or thinking. We learn to label and define. We learn that we have to choose between being a doctor or an artist, an attorney or a musician, a web programmer or a chef.

We are brainwashed to believe that in order to enjoy financial abundance, we must work faster, harder, and be more analytical and more educated than the next guy. Unfortunately, we subconsciously carry this mindset with us into adulthood. We believe that if we are a musician, artist, teacher, poet, or any other professional who leverages more right brain qualities, our lives will be rich with empathy, purpose, culture, love, meaningful relationships, and good health. But, we will likely end up flat broke.

Alternatively, if we become a leader, executive, or other businessperson, we will prosper economically. But, we will pay a price in our personal lives. Our lives will lack purpose, our relationships will be empty, our health will be compromised due to stress, and we will have little to no intuition or empathy.

This is the Tyranny of Or, and we must come to realize that separation is an illusion.

Whether or not we consciously recognize it, we are each a balance of creativity and accuracy. We are artistic and logical, open-minded and detail-oriented. Each of us is the artist and the logical thinker, empathic and cerebral, brain and brawn. We bring our best into the world when we simultaneously toggle back and forth between the two. This integration of self is what our businesses, relationships, and the world need.

THERE IS POWER IN INTEGRATION

Consider the thought, I need more work-life balance. Is work not life? It's not like you leave your life to go to work. Inherent in the term is the notion that they are two separate things. In your life, you do certain things, one of them being work. There is no such thing as work-life balance; there is just balance. The same reasoning applies to business. It's not about balancing profit and purpose. We need to seamlessly integrate both. If we don't do something about it, separation will be the death of our business. When we don't integrate, we miss opportunities by not connecting authentically with our consumer. We fail to see ways we can enhance our brand and products if we are being too linear. In this day and age, when we ignore what our communities are yearning for—soul, purpose, and passion—we become overworked, stressed out, tired, and our businesses suffer.

What could it mean for us if more leaders embraced And? Purpose And Profit. We don't have to give up one for the other. We need to ask ourselves the following questions: Do we have good relationships with our staff and provide value to our customers? Is our business serving humanity? Are we connecting with our consumers in an authentic and meaningful way? Are we delivering value and purpose?

In *Red Goldfish*, Stan Phelps and Graeme Newell make the case that business needs to evolve into a purpose-first mindset. They demonstrate how companies can embrace both purpose **And** profit. The book underscores that actions speak louder than words. Businesses need to do the little things (Red Goldfish) to bring purpose to life.

INTRODUCTION

BY STAN PHELPS

"The true lover of knowledge naturally strives for truth, and is not content with common opinion, but soars with undimmed and unwearied passion till he grasps the essential nature of things."

– Plato

It was the spring of 2013 and my first year as an entrepreneur. I had been introduced to S. Chris Edmonds by a mutual friend. I mentioned to Chris that I was working on launching my business as an author, keynote speaker, and workshop facilitator. He recommended that I speak to Mark Levy.

Mark Levy leads a consulting practice called Levy Innovation, which is focused on positioning. Described as the "horse whisperer" for writers, Levy has worked with prominent thought leaders such as Marshall Goldsmith, Simon Sinek, David Meerman Scott, and Cali Yost. I hired Mark to help me develop my platform. Over six weeks, he coached me on creating marketplace differentiation, crafting an elevator pitch, mining my backstory, and developing a go-to-market strategy.

Mark is brilliant. He taught me a great deal about understanding my big idea and the importance of backstory. We spent a considerable amount of time on not only the what and how, but also the why. To illustrate the importance of communicating my why, Mark shared a story about one of his clients. It was one I'd never forget.

THE POWER OF PURPOSE

The client was a financial planner for small business owners. Let's call him Ed. Ed had shared with Mark that he recruited the majority of his new clients by speaking. He would give a 90-minute seminar on managing finances. At the end of the seminar, Ed would offer a free one-hour consultation/assessment. If there were 40 people in the room, he'd typically have only two or three take him up on the offer. The need to grow his client base led him to Mark. As they began to work together, Mark asked Ed why he chose to pursue a career in accounting. Ed shared that the inspiration began during his teenage years. His parents had passed away in a car accident, and he had been raised by his grandparents. His grandfather had worked at a local company for over 30 years. His grandmother was working as an office administrative assistant in a local school. Ed could remember sitting in his living room at age 14 like it was yesterday. His grandfather was next to him reading the newspaper. An advertisement caught his grandfather's eye. The ad was for the sale of a local butcher shop. He approached his wife and expressed his desire to purchase the business. They both would quit their jobs and go into the business for themselves. His wife was skeptical, but eventually agreed.

Ed watched his grandparents cash in their life savings to start their new business. The butcher shop didn't make any money the first year, lost money in its second year, and a little more in year three. By the end of the fifth year, they had lost their remaining capital and were forced to close the business. Instead of enjoying their retirement, his grandparents went back to full-time jobs and both worked until they passed away. Ed shared that he went into accounting because he didn't want other small business owners to experience what had happened to his grandparents. Mark asked Ed to share this personal backstory during his next seminar. The results were staggering. Ed merely told his backstory on why he became a financial planner before starting his regular session. At the end, he made his usual pitch. 37 out of the 40 attendees took him up on the offer, many of whom became clients for Ed.

ARRIVING AT THE ULTIMATE DIFFERENTIATOR

I began writing back in 2008. I spent a year blogging about 50 different topics in marketing. I was searching for what I thought would be a game changer in business. The following year I had a "moment of truth" in New York City that changed my life. It was a summer evening and I was with a work colleague. Brad and I were at a trendy rooftop bar; it was one of those places where a bottle of beer is $15. We were waiting to meet a few people before heading over to a networking event. I noticed an older gentleman sitting on his own. As the minutes passed, it became obvious that he was waiting for someone. I decided to strike up a conversation about waiting by offering my standard line: "Did you know that we spend 10% of our life waiting?" I told him I knew it was true because I once read it online. We laughed and started talking about the etiquette of waiting. I stressed the importance of being on time. Right then, this guy shook his head and said something I'll never forget: "There is no such thing as being on time. Being on time is a fallacy. You either are early... or you are late. No one is ever on time. On time is a myth." This was a complete paradigm shift for me. I immediately starting thinking about how this applied to marketing and meeting customer expectations. I've always thought that the idea of simply meeting expectations was a surefire recipe for losing business. It almost guarantees you will fall short. I walked away from that brief conversation with a new conviction–too much attention was being placed on awareness and acquisition. I believed that successful businesses would need to find the little things to maximize the customer experience by putting customers first. In other words, they needed to take care of the customers they had so those customers would bring them the referred customers they wanted.

I became a disciple of the late Ted Levitt. Levitt believed that business should put the customer at the center of everything they do. Levitt asserted, "The search for meaningful distinction is central to the marketing effort. If marketing is about anything, it is about achieving customer-getting distinction by differentiating what you do and how you operate. All else is derivative of that and only that." I believed the focus of business should be on customers and not just chasing bottom line profits. Profit was the result, not the aim. I believed customer experience would soon become the new marketing.

After collecting over 1,000 examples and writing my first book, *Purple Goldfish*, my thinking was slightly altered. I found that the companies who did a little extra for their customers also applied the same principles for their employees. In fact, many of those successful companies seemed to place a greater emphasis on culture and putting their employees first. It led me to crowdsource another 1,000+ examples. These examples were focused on the little things for employees to help drive engagement and reinforce culture. The result was my second book, *Green Goldfish*.

My outlook after *Green Goldfish* was altered once again. I had previously held the view that you treat all of your customers and all of your employees the same. I came to realize that for most companies, 80% of profitability is created by just 20% of customers. In addition, 80% of the value that is created by a business comes from just 20% of the employees. I realized that you don't treat everyone the same; you treat everyone fairly. My third book in the original trilogy, *Golden Goldfish*, focused on the little things you do for your "vital few" in business.

I now believe there is an ultimate differentiator. While writing *Golden Goldfish*, I was introduced to Chris Malone. Chris Malone co-authored *The Human Brand* with Susan T. Fiske. The book examines the concepts of warmth and competence in relation to business. As humans, our brains are hardwired to sense warmth and competence immediately. Warmth trumps competence. Warmth starts inside your organization and radiates outwards, to your customer. If you want to win the hearts of employees and the wallets of customers, you must go out of your way to put their interests ahead of yours. Malone and Fiske call this the principle of worthy intentions. These worthy intentions are typically linked to the purpose of your company. I now believe that purpose is becoming the ultimate differentiator.

This book will explore how business is evolving, the importance of putting purpose first, how to define your purpose, the eight purpose archetypes, and how to create the little things that bring purpose to life.

PREFACE: PURPOSE BY THE NUMBERS

Here are 10 statistics that make the case for purpose in business:

10. In *Firms of Endearment*, Raj Sisodia looked at 28 public and private companies based on characteristics such as their stated purpose, generosity of compensation, quality of customer service, investment in their communities, and impact on the environment. The eighteen publicly traded companies out of the total 28 companies outperformed the S&P 500 index by a factor of 10.5 over the years 1996-2011[1].

9. 90 percent of executives surveyed said their company understands the importance of purpose, but only 46 percent said it informs their strategic and operational decision-making[2].

8. All things being equal, 86 percent of customers will choose to do business with companies whose values mesh with their own. Source: Brand Fuel

7. 81 percent of manufacturers and 73 percent of retailers acknowledge that environmental and social impact programs are methods of reducing risk[3].

---

1. https://hbr.org/2013/04/companies-that-practice-conscious-capitalism-perform

2. http://www.ey.com/Publication/vwLUAssets/ey-the-business-case-for-purpose/$FILE/ey-the-business-case-for-purpose.pdf

3. http://www.sustainablebrands.com/news_and_views/stakeholder_trends_insights/hannah_furlong/competitiveness_reputation_deliver_higher_ROI

6. 6 out of 7 employees would consider leaving an employer whose values no longer met their expectations[4].

5. 58 percent of companies with a clearly articulated and understood purpose experienced growth of +10%[5].

4. Companies who embrace purpose have a 44 percent higher employee retention rate. Source: Gallup

3. Purpose increases sales by 37 percent. Source: Shawn Achor

2. Purposeful, value-driven companies outperform their counterparts by a factor of 12[6].

1. Capitalism may have the ability to end poverty on Earth. The percentage of people living on less than $1 per day has dropped from 85% in 1820 to 17% in 2003. If current trends continue, poverty will be virtually eliminated in the next 50 years[7].

4. https://www.pwc.com/m1/en/services/consulting/documents/millennials-at-work.pdf

5. https://cdn.imperative.com/media/public/Global_Purpose_Index_2016.pdf

6. https://www.amazon.com/Corporate-Culture-Performance-John-Kotter/dp/1451655320

7. http://www.sandermahieu.com/wp-content/uploads/2015/03/Raj-Sisodia-Conscious-Capitalism-Presentation-BVC-South-Africa.pdf

PART I

WHAT IS A RED
GOLDFISH?

CHAPTER 1

THE EVOLUTION
OF BUSINESS

"Consumers want a better world,
not just better widgets."

—Simon Mainwaring

Why are we here? This is perhaps the greatest question of all. It has been pondered since the earliest days of human existence. It is our search for meaning in this world. Each one of us is challenged with answering this question. Mark Twain once said that the two most important days in our lives are the day we are born and the day we find out why. Should the "why" question apply to business?

Why are companies in business? What or who comes first in business? Where is its main focus? We believe there are four schools of thought.

We'll call the first school of thought the 1.0 version.

BUSINESS 1.0 - SHAREHOLDER FIRST

> *"There is one and only one social responsibility of business*
> *and that is to engage in activities designed to increase profits."*

> - Milton Friedman

The 1.0 version of the evolution of business was a shareholder first mindset. The sole purpose of a company was to maximize profits. The late economist Milton Friedman became its foremost proponent. He famously shared in his 1970 *New York Times* article that, "there is one and only one social responsibility of business–to use its resources and engage in activities designed to increase its profits so long as it stays within the rules of the game, which is to say, engages in open and free competition without deception or fraud."

Profit was the coveted prize of business. Friedman excoriated leaders who sought anything beyond profits as "unwitting puppets of the intellectual forces that have been undermining the basis of a free society." Business leaders who pursued social interests were guilty of spending money that wasn't their own. Friedman branded them as "unelected government officials" who were illegally tax-ing employers and customers. The simple goal of business was to provide a return to shareholders. By focusing on external social responsibilities or lofty ideals, business is distracted from its sole purpose of maximizing profits.

Friedman believed that doing good was incompatible with doing well for your shareholders. Over the last two decades, this view has been changing. "There is an increasing awareness that the purpose of a company has to go beyond shareholder value, and that this is not something that will cost your business but something that will enhance your business," said Michael Beer, Cahners-Rabb Professor of Business Administration, Emeritus, at Harvard Business School.

The next evolution of business put the focus squarely on customers first.

BUSINESS 2.0 - CUSTOMER FIRST

*"Not so long ago companies assumed the purpose of a business
is to make money. But that has proved as vacuous as saying
the purpose of life is to eat...The purpose of a business is to create and
keep a customer."*

- Ted Levitt

The 2.0 version of business sees profit as an end result, not the goal. Companies should be dedicated to the business of getting and keep-ing customers. This focus places importance on the overall custom-er experience and managing ongoing relationships. In the words of Walmart's founder, Sam Walton, "There is only one boss. The cus-tomer. And he can fire everybody in the company from the chair-man on down, simply by spending his money somewhere else."

The late Ted Levitt believed that companies should stop defining themselves by what they produce. Instead they should reorient themselves toward customer needs. In his best-known *Harvard Business Review* article, "Marketing Myopia," Levitt made the case for companies focusing on customers. He used the railroad industry to illustrate the point.

> The railroads did not stop growing because the need for passenger and freight transportation declined. That grew. The railroads are in trouble today not because that need was filled by others (cars, trucks, airplanes, and even telephones) but because it was not filled by the railroads themselves. They let others take customers away from them because they assumed themselves to be in the railroad business rather than in the transportation business. The reason they defined their industry incorrectly was that they were railroad-oriented instead of transportation-oriented; they were product-oriented instead of customer-oriented[1].

Want an example of a company that puts its customers first? Look no further than Amazon. It's the focus of their mission: "We seek to be Earth's most customer-centric company." Founder Jeff Bezos puts customers first and profit second. "We're not competitor obsessed, we're customer obsessed. We start with the customer and we work backwards...We've had three big ideas at Amazon that we've stuck with for 18 years, and they're the reason we're successful: Put the customer first. Invent. And be patient." says Bezos.

This obsession with customers dates back to the earliest days of Amazon. There is always an empty chair in company meetings. The chair at the table represents the customer. The message is clear; the

---

1. https://hbr.org/2006/10/what-business-are-you-in-classic-advice-from-theodore-levitt

current customer is always top of mind and seen as the most important person in the room.

Peter Drucker made a similar argument for a customer-first focus in his classic book, *Management*, when he wrote, "There is only one valid definition of business purpose: to create a customer... It is the customer who determines what a business is. It is the customer alone whose willingness to pay for a good or for a service converts economic resources into wealth, things into goods...The customer is the foundation of a business and keeps it in existence."

The next version of business put employees and culture at the forefront.

BUSINESS 3.0 - EMPLOYEE FIRST

"Employees First, Customers Second is a management approach. It is a philosophy, a set of ideas, a way of looking at strategy and competitive advantage."

– Vineet Nayar, Former CEO of HCL Technologies

The 3.0 version of business places employees first. It's rooted in understanding where value is created in an organization. It's created in the last two feet of a transaction, the space between the employee and the customer. Former HCL Technologies CEO Vineet Nayar calls these 24 inches the "value zone." Nayar made employees the priority at HCL, putting employees first, customers second, management third, and shareholders last. He believed front line employees were the true custodians of the brand and drivers of customer loyalty. Nayar wanted to shift the focus from the "WHAT" of what HCL offered, to the "HOW" of delivering value.

A focus on employees first is based on the idea that culture trumps strategy in an organization. The experience of your employees becomes paramount as it dictates your overall culture. "I came to see in my time at IBM that 'culture' isn't just one aspect of the game–it is the game." says Lou Gerstner, Former IBM CEO and author of *Who Says Elephants Can't Dance*.

In today's workplace, up to 70% of workers are either not engaged or are actively disengaged. To be successful, you need employees who are engaged to create a strong customer experience. According to Ted Coiné, author of *Five Star Customer Service*, "You can't create happy enthused customers without happy engaged employees."

The next evolution of business places purpose as the critical first piece of the puzzle.

BUSINESS 4.0 - PURPOSE FIRST

"On the face of it, shareholder value is the dumbest idea in the world...
Shareholder value is a result, not a strategy...
Your main constituencies are your employees,
your customers and your products "

- Jack Welch, Former CEO of GE

The 4.0 version of business places purpose first. Companies that have a strong, defined purpose find that it drives employee engagement, connects with customers, and fuels the bottom line. According to Deloitte Global CEO Punit Renjen, "Exceptional firms have always been good at aligning their purpose with their execution, and as a result have enjoyed category leadership in sales and profits." John Kotter and James Heskett demonstrated in their book *Corporate Culture & Performance*, that purposeful, value-driven companies outperform their counterparts in stock price by a factor of 12.

Purpose relates to your "Why" as a business. To quote Simon Sinek, "People don't buy what you do or how you do it, they buy why you do it." It should permeate everything you do. "Every decision should be looked at in terms of purpose. Some decisions may be purpose neutral. But purpose is certainly not just a marketing issue or positioning of your brand image. Purpose should impact every aspect of the firm," says Raj Sisodia, author of *Conscious Capitalism* and FW Olin Distinguished Professor of Global Business at Babson College.

Embracing purpose can become a driver of employee engagement. Daniel Pink touched on the importance of purpose in his book *Drive*. Pink said there are three things that motivate people: autonomy, mastery, and purpose. He believes that purpose is perhaps the greatest of the three, because a strong purpose allows you to overcome obstacles and persevere towards a goal.

A NEW WAY FORWARD

The old view of business was a profit-first mindset. You put shareholders first, customers second, employees third, and purpose fourth in terms of focus.

The new view of business going forward calls for a purpose-first mindset. It is the exact opposite of the traditional approach. You put purpose at the center of everything the business does. Then, employees come second and customers third. Taking care of those three, sustainable profit becomes the result as opposed to the sole aim.

CHAPTER 2

THE BLURRING OF LINES

"Well-run, values-centered businesses can contribute to humankind in more tangible ways than any other organization in society."

—Bill George, former CEO of Medtronic

Purpose is changing the way we work and do business for the foreseeable future. It is our belief that by 2020, there will no longer be a distinction between for-profit companies and non-profit organizations. The evolution of the corporate social responsibility, benefit corporations, new non-profit models, and the conscious capitalism movement have forever blurred the line of how we look at businesses.

The traditional view of business was binary. A distinction between companies was made based on corporate filing status. You were either a for-profit corporation or a non-profit organization.

OLD VIEW - BINARY BASED ON CORPORATE FILING STATUS

NON-PROFIT 501(c)3 <————> FOR-PROFIT C CORP

Today the lines are not so clear. There are variations of both non-profit and for-profit businesses. The emergence of social media has increased transparency in business. It has shined a light on the intentions of organizations. Purpose is now becoming a differentiator. Beyond products and features, consumers now want to know the "why" behind a company.

NEW PARADIGM - HYBRID BASED ON THE COMBINATION OF PROFIT AND PURPOSE

FOR-PURPOSE <————> NOT-FOR-PURPOSE

Let's look at the variations between a not-for-purpose organization and a for-purpose organization:

For-Profits [High Profit, Low Purpose] - For-profit describes a business that is owned and controlled by its members. These mem-

FOR-PURPOSE MATRIX

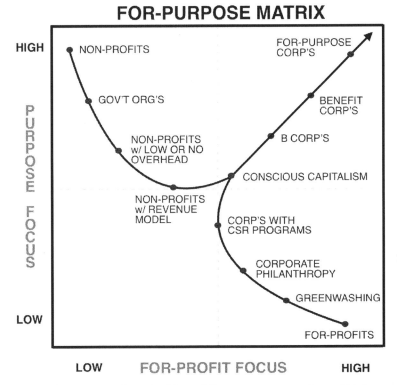

bers are known as shareholders. The percentage of profits for each shareholder is determined by the portion of shares in the company that they own.

Non-Profits [Low Profit, High Purpose] - Non-profit describes a business that is formed in furtherance of a purpose. They do not seek profit. In the US, these organizations must be approved by the Internal Revenue Service to be tax-exempt under the terms of section 501(c)(3) of the Internal Revenue Code. The code dictates that tax-exemptions can apply to entities that are organized and operated exclusively for religious, charitable, scientific, literary, or educational purposes, or for testing for public safety, or to foster national or international amateur sports competition, or for the prevention of cruelty to children or animals.

Greenwashing [High Profit, Low Purpose] - Whitewashing is a coordinated attempt to hide unpleasant facts, typically in a political context. Greenwashing is the same premise but in an environmental context in business. Greenwashing is when a company or organization spends more time and money claiming to be "green" through advertising and marketing than actually implementing business practices that minimize environmental impact[1].

Government Organizations [Low to Moderate Profit, Moderate Purpose] - Government organizations refer to businesses that are created by the state or a public body. These organizations are frequently managed and operated as joint-stock corporations with the government owning either all or a controlling stake of the shares. This form is often referred to as a state-owned enterprise. A state-owned enterprise might variously operate as a not-for-profit corporation, as it may not be required to generate a profit; as a commercial enterprise in competitive sectors; or as a natural monopoly. If profitable, governments may also use these organizations to support the general budget.

Corporate Philanthropy [High Profit, Low to Moderate Purpose] - Corporate philanthropy is the act of a corporation or business promoting the welfare of others, generally via charitable donations of funds or time. Charity and philanthropy are often used interchangeably, however, this should not be the case. According to *Philanthropy in America: A History*, the difference between the two is that "charity relieves the pains of social problems, whereas philanthropy attempts to solve these problems at their root." Corporate philanthropy is often focused on treating the issues that non-profit organizations exist to serve. Corporate philanthropy can come through a variety of channels – monetary donations or gifts of time and talent (in-kind donations). Commonly, these may be matching

---

1. http://greenwashingindex.com/about-greenwashing/

gifts, volunteer grants, and any other type of product or service donation that is non-monetary.

Non-Profits with Low or No Overhead [Moderate Profit, High Purpose] - Donors tend to avoid charities that dedicate a high percentage of expenses to administrative and fundraising costs. The perceived reason is that high overhead limits the ability of a non-profit to be effective. Non-profits with low or no overhead enjoy a more sustainable model than their traditional non-profit counterparts.

Corporations with CSR Programs [High to Moderate Profit, Moderate Purpose] - Corporate Social Responsibility (CSR) is a concept whereby companies integrate social and environmental concerns in their business operations and in their interactions with their stakeholders on a voluntary basis. This happens when organizations go beyond minimum legal requirements and obligations to address societal needs. CSR is a form of corporate self-regulation integrated into a business model. The aim is to increase long-term profits and shareholder trust through positive public relations and high ethical standards to reduce business and legal risk by taking responsibility for corporate actions. CSR strategies encourage the company to make a positive impact on the environment and stakeholders including consumers, employees, investors, communities, and others[2].

Non-Profit with a Revenue Model [Moderate Profit, Moderate to High Purpose] - Non-profits are starting to blend social mission and commercial enterprise. As government funding sources have dried up and competition for foundation grants has gotten more intense, non-profits are starting to embrace earned revenue opportunities[3].

---

2. http://digitalcommons.liberty.edu/cgi/viewcontent.cgi?article=1229&context=honors

3. http://nonprofithub.org/starting-a-nonprofit/%E2%80%9Cthe-hybrid-ideal%E2%80%9D%E2%80%94john-fulwider-on-the-potential-of-nonprofits-with-for-profit-business-models/

Conscious Capitalism [Moderate to High Profit, Moderate to High Purpose] - Conscious Capitalism is a term created by John Mackey and Raj Sisodia. It is a global movement to elevate humanity and awaken the heroic spirit of business. The idea is based on the notion that capitalism can be a force both for economic and social good. There are four components to Conscious Capitalism.

1. Higher Purpose - Conscious Businesses focus on their purpose beyond profit.

2. Stakeholder Integration - Conscious Businesses focus on their whole business ecosystem, creating and optimizing value for all of their stakeholders. Conscious Business is a win-win-win proposition as it includes a healthy return to shareholders.

3. Conscious Leadership - Conscious Leaders focus on "we," rather than "me." They inspire, foster transformation, and bring out the best in those around them. They recognize the integral role of culture and purposefully cultivate a Conscious Culture of trust and care.

4. Conscious Culture - Culture is the embodied values, principles, and practices underlying the social fabric of a business, which permeate its actions and connects the stakeholders to each other and to the company's purpose, people, and processes[4].

B Corp Certification [Moderate to High Profit, Moderate to High Purpose] - B Corp certification is a third party certification by B Lab. The certification is based on the following key items: measurable social performance, accountability, transparency, and measurable environmental performance. The B Corp designation was established in Wayne, Pennsylvania by B Lab co-founders Jay Coen Gilbert and Bart Houlahan. The pair previously ran the athletic footwear/apparel company And 1 in the 1990s and early 2000s.

---

4. https://hbr.org/2013/04/companies-that-practice-conscious-capitalism-perform

They introduced the certified B Corp standard in 2007. The B Corp is a voluntary certification and can be dropped at any time.

There are fees involved with certification as well as future audits to insure compliance with all of its standards.

Benefit Corporations [Moderate to High Profit, Moderate to High Purpose] - A benefit corporation is a true legal entity classification for a for-profit business. Social entrepreneurs can choose this classification to mirror their desires for fiduciary and environmental responsibility. Benefit corporations must commit to the following: "Making a material positive impact on society and the environment[5]." The legal documents utilized in creating this type of corporation are required to consider the consequences of all key actions as they affect stakeholders, not just shareholders. All existing corporate laws still pertain and leadership must still report on the corporation's efforts via current third-party standards. There are currently 31 states that have enacted laws to recognize a benefit corporation. Another seven states are currently working on legislation for it[6].

For-Purpose Corporations [High Profit, High Purpose] - For-purpose is our term for corporations who have purpose ingrained into their business model. These hybrid businesses are not based on an "OR" scenario. They have decided not to choose profit OR purpose. For-purpose companies embrace the power of "AND." They offer both value and meaning. They operate with both analytics and artistry. In the words of David Howitt, author of *Heed Your Call,* "By doing both they are helping to develop the full potential of capitalism, and they are beginning to repair the world."

---

5. https://bloomerang.co/blog/benefit-corporation-vs-certified-b-corp-in-plain-english/
6. http://benefitcorp.net/policymakers/state-by-state-status

CHAPTER 3

PURPOSE IS THE
NEW BLACK

*"Corporate purpose is at the confluence of strategy and values.
It expresses the company's fundamental - the raison d'être or overriding
reason for existing. It is the end to which the strategy is directed."*

—Richard Ellsworth

Purpose is becoming the new black. We believe it's more than a trend or passing fad. Purpose is emerging as a guiding light that can help business navigate and thrive in the 21st century. According to the EY Beacon Institute Pursuit of Purpose Study, "Purpose — an aspirational reason for being that is grounded in humanity — is at the core of how many companies are responding to the business and societal challenges of today."

What can happen if you put purpose at the core of your business? Here are 10 benefits from the EY Purpose Study[7]:

- Purpose instills strategic clarity.

- Purpose guides both short-term decisions and long-term strategy at every level of an organization, encouraging leaders to think about systems holistically.

- Purpose guides choices about what not to do as well as what to do.

- Purpose channels innovation.

- Purpose is a force for and a response to transformation.

- Purpose motivates people through meaning, not fear. It clarifies the long-term outcome so people understand the need for change rather than feeling it is imposed upon them.

- Purpose is also a response to societal pressures on businesses to transform, to address global challenges, and to take a longer-term, more comprehensive approach to growth and value.

- Purpose taps a universal need to contribute, to feel like a part of society.

7. http://www.ey.com/Publication/vwlUAssets/EY-pursuit-of-purpose-exec-sum/$FILE/EY-pursuit-of-purpose-exec-sum.pdf

- Purpose recognizes differences and diversity. Purpose builds bridges.

- Purpose helps individuals/teams to work across silos to pursue a single, compelling aim.

WIN-WIN-WIN

Companies that have a defined purpose benefit from a win-win-win scenario. By standing for something bigger than their products/services, they are winning on three levels:

Win #1: Employees - Purpose helps attract the best talent, keeps them engaged, and retains them. It is important to employees. It helps determine the values of an organization. According to Price-WaterhouseCoopers: 6 out of 7 employees would consider leaving an employer whose values no longer met their expectations[8].

Win #2: Customers – Purpose becomes a differentiator that drives acquisition and retention. It also helps the business stay competitive. It provides a reason for their customers to engage with the business. Purpose is important to customers as it showcases the values of an organization. According to Brand Fuel: All things being equal, 6 out of 7 customers will choose to do business with companies whose values mesh with their own.

Win #3: Shareholders - Purpose has positive effects on key performance drivers. Research shows that companies who clearly articulate their purpose enjoy higher growth rates than non-for-purpose competitors.

---

8. https://www.pwc.com/m1/en/services/consulting/documents/millennials-at-work.pdf

BRINGING PURPOSE TO LIFE

According to Gallup, when it comes to communicating an organization's purpose to your employees, customers, and stakeholders, words don't matter nearly as much as actions do. Companies need to find ways to bring purpose to life. Creating little things that can make a big difference for both employees and customers is one way to bring purpose to life. "It's easy to state a purpose and state a set of values. It's much harder to enact them in the organization because it requires you to continually search for consistency across many disciplines and many activities," says Michael Beer. We call the little things that can be done to bring purpose to life Red Goldfish. In the next two chapters, we will explain the meaning behind this term, including why red and why a goldfish.

CHAPTER 4

WHY A GOLDFISH?

"Big doors swing on little hinges"

— W. Clement Stone

The origin of the goldfish in *Red Goldfish* dates back to 2009 when the Purple Goldfish crowdsourcing project began. It has become the signature element of the book series. A goldfish represents something small, but despite its size, something with the ability to make a big difference.

The inspiration for the goldfish came from Kimpton Hotels. In 2001, the boutique hotel chain's Hotel Monaco began offering travelers a temporary travel companion for the duration of their stay. Perhaps the guests were traveling on business and getting a little lonely. Or maybe were with family and missing the family pet. Whatever the case, Kimpton came to the rescue. Kimpton guests can temporarily adopt a goldfish for their stay. They call the program Guppy Love. The goldfish has now become a signature element of the Kimpton experience with the program attracting national attention.

"The Guppy Love program is a fun extension of our pet-friendly nature as well as our emphasis on indulging the senses to heighten the travel experience," says Steve Pinetti, Senior Vice President of Sales & Marketing for Kimpton Hotels and Restaurants. "Everything about Hotel Monaco appeals directly to the senses, and 'Guppy Love' offers one more unique way to relax, indulge and promote health of mind, body and spirit in our home-away-from-home atmosphere."

Guppy Love inspired the start of the Purple Goldfish Project. Three years later in 2012, the book *Purple Goldfish* was published. This Amazon Bestseller was followed by *Green Goldfish* in 2013 and *Golden Goldfish* in 2014. *Blue Goldfish* became the fourth color in the series in 2016.

The size of a goldfish is relevant to the series. The overarching concept is the idea that littlest things can make the biggest difference. The growth of a goldfish became a metaphor for business. The average common goldfish is between three and four inches in

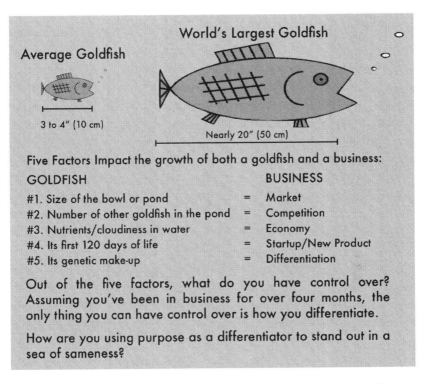

Average Goldfish

3 to 4" (10 cm)

World's Largest Goldfish

Nearly 20" (50 cm)

Five Factors Impact the growth of both a goldfish and a business:

GOLDFISH		BUSINESS
#1. Size of the bowl or pond	=	Market
#2. Number of other goldfish in the pond	=	Competition
#3. Nutrients/cloudiness in water	=	Economy
#4. Its first 120 days of life	=	Startup/New Product
#5. Its genetic make-up	=	Differentiation

Out of the five factors, what do you have control over? Assuming you've been in business for over four months, the only thing you can have control over is how you differentiate.

How are you using purpose as a differentiator to stand out in a sea of sameness?

The growth of a goldfish and the growth of a business are affected by the following five factors:

#1. SIZE OF THE BOWL OR POND = THE MARKET

GROWTH FACTOR: The size of the bowl or pond.

RULE OF THUMB: Direct correlation. The larger the bowl or pond, the larger the goldfish can grow. The smaller the market, the smaller the business growth opportunity.

#2. NUMBER OF OTHER GOLDFISH IN THE POND = COMPETITION

GROWTH FACTOR: The number of goldfish in the same bowl or pond.

RULE OF THUMB: Inverse correlation. The more goldfish, the less growth. The less competition, the more business growth opportunity.

#3. NUTRIENTS AND CLOUDINESS OF THE WATER = THE ECONOMY

GROWTH FACTOR: The cloudiness of the water and the level of nutrients in the water.

RULE OF THUMB: Direct correlation. The more nutrients and better clarity, the larger the growth. The less access to capital or reduced consumer confidence, the more difficult it is for a business to grow.

> **FACT**
>
> A malnourished goldfish in a crowded, cloudy environment may only grow to two inches (five centimeters).

#4. ITS FIRST 120 DAYS OF LIFE = STARTUP PHASE OR PRODUCT LAUNCH

GROWTH FACTOR: The nourishment and treatment they receive as a baby goldfish.

RULE OF THUMB: Direct correlation. The lower the quality of the food, water, and treatment, the more the goldfish will be stunted for future growth. The stronger the leadership and capital as a start-up, the better the business growth.

FACT

A baby goldfish is called a fry. They are tiny when they are born, literally a "small fry."

#5. ITS GENETIC MAKEUP = DIFFERENTIATION

GROWTH FACTOR: The genetic makeup of the goldfish.

RULE OF THUMB: Direct correlation. The weaker the genes or the less differentiated, the less the goldfish can grow. The more differentiated the product or service from the competition, the better the chance for business growth.

FACT

The current *Guinness Book of World Records* holder for the largest goldfish hails from The Netherlands at a whopping 19 inches (50 centimeters). To put that in perspective, that's about the size of the average domestic cat.

WHICH OF THE FIVE FACTORS CAN YOU CONTROL?

Let's assume you have an existing product or service and have been in business for more than four months. Do you have any control over the market, your competition, or the economy? NO, NO and NO. The only thing you have control over is your business' genetic makeup or how you differentiate your product or service.

It is our belief that purpose is becoming the ultimate differentiator. How are you leveraging becoming for-purpose in your business? In goldfish terms, how are you standing out in a sea of sameness?

CHAPTER 5

WHY RED?

*"We picked up one excellent word - a word
worth traveling to New Orleans to get;
a nice limber, expressive, handy word—lagniappe"*

— Mark Twain

Red is the fifth color in the Goldfish series of books. The initial colored trilogy of books was an ode to an iconic American city and its most famous event. That city is New Orleans. Purple, green, and gold are the three official colors of Mardi Gras. It's a reference to New Orleans because there is one word from New Orleans that exemplifies the concept of doing little extra. That word is lagniappe. Pronounced lan-yap, it is a creole word meaning an "added gift" or "to give more." The practice originated in Louisiana in the 1840's, whereby a merchant would give a customer a little something extra at the time of purchase. It is a signature personal touch by the business that creates goodwill and promotes word of mouth.

According to Webster's:

LAGNIAPPE (lanʹyəəp, lăn-yăpʹ) *Chiefly Southern Louisiana & Mississippi*

> 1. A small gift presented by a store owner to a customer with the customer's purchase.
>
> 2. An extra or unexpected gift or benefit. Also called boot.

Mark Twain was smitten with the word. He wrote about lagniappe in the book *Life on the Mississippi*:

> We picked up one excellent word–a word worth traveling to New Orleans to get; a nice limber, expressive, handy word–"lagniappe." They pronounce it lanny-yap. It is Spanish–so they said. We discovered it at the head of a column of odds and ends in the [Times] Picayune [newspaper] the first day; heard twenty people use it the second; inquired what it meant the third; adopted it and got facility in swinging it the fourth. It

has a restricted meaning, but I think the people spread it out a little when they choose. It is the equivalent of the thirteenth roll in a baker's dozen. It is something thrown in, gratis, for good measure. The custom originated in the Spanish quarter of the city.

In the trilogy, *Purple Goldfish* focused on the little things you could do to improve the customer experience, *Green Goldfish* examined how to drive engagement to improve the employee experience, and the third book, *Golden Goldfish,* uncovered the importance of taking care of your best customers/employees.

The fourth book, *Blue Goldfish,* revealed how to leverage technology, data, and analytics to improve the customer experience. Blue was a reference to a 10th century Danish king named Harald Gormsson. Gormsson united Scandinavia and converted the Danes to Christianity. His nickname was Bluetooth, a reference to a dead tooth that had turned blue. In the 1990's, Bluetooth became the name for the wireless area networking standard we use today. Blue highlights convergence, just as Bluetooth was the result of a consortium and King Harald united Scandinavia. Our convergence is big data and little data coming together to deliver high-level personalized experiences.

WHY RED?

Red is the color of blood. It's been historically been associated with sacrifice and courage. In the US and Europe, red also represents passion, whereas in Asia, it symbolizes happiness and good fortune. We, however, went farther afield for our source. Our inspiration for red comes from Africa.

(RED) was created by Bono and Bobby Shriver. Launched at the World Economic Forum in 2006, its purpose was to engage the private sector and its marketing prowess in order to raise funds for the fight against AIDS in Africa. On the back of a napkin, they outlined their idea for a unique union of brands and consumers. The plan had three goals:

1. Provide consumers with a choice that made giving effortless.

2. Generate profits and a sense of purpose for partner companies.

3. Create a source of sustainable income for the Global Fund to fund the fight against AIDS[9].

(RED) was a continuation of work for Africa by U2's lead singer. In 2002, Bono co-founded DATA (Debt, AIDS, Trade, Africa), a platform to raise public awareness of the issues in its name and influence government policy on Africa. In 2004, DATA helped to create ONE: The Campaign to Make Poverty History. ONE is dedicated to fighting extreme poverty and preventable disease. In early 2008, DATA and ONE combined operations under the ONE organization.

(RED) has a clear purpose in its manifesto:

> Every Generation is known for something.
>
> Let's be the one to deliver an AIDS FREE GENERATION.
>
> We all have tremendous power. What we choose to do or even buy, can affect someone's life on the other side of the world. In 2005, more than 1,200 babies were born every day with HIV. Today that number is 400. We must act now to get that close to zero.

---

9. http://www.wolffolins.com/work/37/red

(RED) can't accomplish this alone. It will take all of us to get there —governments, health organizations, companies, and you. When you BUY (RED), a (RED) partner will give up some of its profits to fight AIDS.

It's as simple as that.

BE (RED). Start the end of AIDS now.

Prior to the launch of (RED), businesses had contributed just $5 million to the Global Fund in four years. In the decade since its inception, the private sector, through (RED), has contributed over $350 million. One hundred percent of the funds are invested in HIV/AIDS programs in Africa with a focus on countries with high prevalence of mother-to-child transmission of HIV.

The branding agency Wolff Olins helped build the platform for (RED). They created a unique brand architecture that united participating businesses by literally multiplying their logos to the power (RED).

Global brands such as Apple, Nike, Dell, American Express, and The Gap came on board. The appeal of (RED) was clear: it allowed them to tap into a purpose beyond their own profit. Partner brands created special (RED) versions of products and a portion of the profits from the sales would contribute to the Global Fund to fight malaria, tuberculosis, and AIDS.

Here are some examples of (RED) initiatives:

- American Express offers a Red card.

- Gap sells a line of merchandise including T-shirts, jackets, scarves, gloves, jewelry, bags, and purses called Product Red. Gap donates 50% of all Product Red profits directly to the Global Fund.

- Converse is selling a shoe made from African mud cloth.

- Apple Inc. has released special edition iPod Touch 5th generation and five other generations of iPod Nano and the iPod Shuffle with a Product (RED) theme, as well as a (RED) $25 iTunes Gift Card. They have also released Product (RED) branded Smart Covers and Smart Cases for the iPad 2, iPad (3rd generation), iPad (4th generation), iPad Air, iPad Mini, and a leather case for the iPhone 5S.

- Nike has released a special line of red shoelaces with the profit going to the charity. Their motto is "Lace up, save lives." Didier Drogba is the face for the promotion of the laces.

- Hallmark has introduced greeting cards that are Product Red.

- In a partnership with Microsoft, Dell announced that it would manufacture versions of its computers (XPS One, XPS M1530, and XPS M1530) that would come with a PRODUCT (RED) version of Windows Vista Ultimate preinstalled. The company also released a PRODUCT (RED) printer.

- Starbucks participated during their 2008 holiday promotion. For every holiday beverage ordered, 5 cents went to PRODUCT (RED). Starbucks also offers the Red Card and donates five cents every time the card is used.

- The band The Killers writes a Christmas song every year in aid of RED. Profits are given to the charity.

- Monster Cable makes a special edition Beats by Dr. Dre Solo HD with the name Solo HD (PRODUCT)RED.

- Belvedere vodka produces special edition red-colored bottles. A portion of the proceeds go to (PRODUCT)RED.

- In 2014, U2 released a charity single "Invisible" and a Super Bowl commercial to announce the partnership between RED and Bank of America.

(RED) helped reinforce the simple idea that doing good is good business for both customers and employees. American Express saw an immediate lift in brand perception with younger customers, while GAP saw a major improvement in employee engagement as well as the quality of incoming recruits. Their INSPI(RED) T-shirt became the biggest seller in their history.

Starbucks was one of the very first (RED) partners. Here is how they describe the relationship:

We have deep relationships with many coffee-growing communities in Africa. Their health and prosperity are important to us, and we have an opportunity to help them thrive, and to use our size for good. One way we support our global communities is through our eight-year partnership with (RED) – thanks to you we've contributed more than $14 million and counting. All donations generated through (STARBUCKS) RED campaigns have gone to the Global Fund to help finance HIV/AIDS prevention, education and treatment programs.

The program is making a difference.

There have been enormous gains in the fight against AIDS in the last decade, but also persistent challenges. We believe the elimination of mother to child transmissions by 2020 and the end of AIDS as a public health threat by 2030 is possible, but only with continued funding and focus. Without these efforts, the epidemic threatens to outpace the response and undo the progress that's been achieved[10].

---

10. https://www.starbucks.com/responsibility/community/starbucks-red

The (RED) movement uses the symbolism of red as the color of emergency. The organization believes the AIDS pandemic is an emergency. In 2010, (RED) lit up more than 90 landmarks on World Aids Day. The purpose was to shine a red light on the 37 million people around the world living with HIV. Starting in Australia, U2 helped light the Sydney Opera House (RED). Soon the Tokyo Tower and Table Mountain in Cape Town were glowing (RED) too. Sienna Miller turned the London Eye (RED), and Penelope Cruz turned the Empire State Building (RED) in New York City. Even the dome of St. Paul's Cathedral in Rome turned (RED).

In the words of Wolff Olins, "The appeal of (RED) was clear: it connected these corporations with a purpose beyond their own profit. Some partners went as far as manufacturing products or packaging in African countries, generating jobs, and opportunities for local people[11]."

Today, a quarter of all international funding for HIV/AIDS-related programs, over half for tuberculosis, and almost three-quarters for malaria worldwide comes from The Global Fund. 100% of the funds generated by (RED) partners and events goes to Global Fund programs that provide medical care and support services for people affected by HIV/AIDS in Africa. No overhead is taken by either (RED) or the Global Fund. (RED) is the largest private sector donor to the Global Fund and has generated hundreds of millions in funding for HIV/AIDS programs in Africa.

The (RED) campaign inspired this book. Red represents the simple idea that brands can be a force for good in the world. They can have a greater purpose beyond striving for profit to always be in the black. We hope to change the meaning behind "being in the red."

---

11. http://www.wolffolins.com/work/37/red

PART II

THE ARCHETYPES

CHAPTER 6

THE ARCHETYPES

"Everything a brand does—from stores to product to packaging to how you feel about that brand—has to be designed."

— Lee Clow, TBWAChiatDay/Los Angeles

We started the Red Goldfish Project in 2015. Since its origination, we've collected information on over 250 companies, specifically looking for ways that brands bring purpose to life. Our research database includes over 700 articles and nearly 3,500 videos. [See the collection of videos searchable by brand, archetype, and chapter at http://602communications.com/RedGoldfish]

In reviewing all of the companies, we began to see patterns. We saw that brands would typically fall into one of eight purpose archetypes:

1. The Protector - "Those who protect what is important."

> Example: Patagonia - their purpose is to help reimagine a sustainable world for those who come after us.

2. The Liberator - "Those who reinvent a broken system."

> Example: Harley Davidson - their purpose is to fulfill dreams of personal freedom through the experience of motorcycling.

3. The Designer - "Those who empower through the creation of revolutionary products."

> Example: Apple - their purpose is to make tools for the mind that advance humankind.

4. The Guide - "Those who help facilitate individual progress."

> Example: Google - their purpose is to organize the world's information and make it universally accessible.

5. The Advocate - "Those who advocate for a tribe."

Example: Panera - their purpose is to help people live consciously and eat deliciously.

6. The Challenger - "Those who inspire people toward transformative action."

Example: Nike - their purpose is to inspire every athlete...and if you have a body, you are an athlete.

7. The Unifier - "Those who command individuals to join a movement."

Example: Whole Foods - their purpose is to set the standards of excellence for food retailers.

8. The Master - "Those on a mission to change lives and improve the world."

Example: Warby Parker - their purpose is to offer designer eyewear at a revolutionary price, while leading the way for socially conscious businesses.

Over the next eight chapters, we'll explore each archetype. In addition, each chapter will share case studies of brands that fit that particular archetype. The case studies we'll share contain three distinct elements:

Purpose Statement - this element is one sentence that describes the purpose of the brand. It will embody the *raison d'etre*, the reason for their existence. Each purpose statement begins with "To."

Note: we were able to find a stated purpose in about two thirds of the brands we studied. In some cases, we extrapolated a purpose statement from our own understanding of the brand.

Backstory - this element will provide a brief history of the brand, with a focus on the founding of the company. Many times the purpose of a business can be tracked to its founders. An understanding of the backstory is critical.

Red Goldfish - this element is where we share an example of how the brand created a program, campaign, or initiative that brought their purpose to life.

HIERARCHY OF NEEDS

The order for the eight archetypes is meaningful. We were inspired by Abraham Maslow's hierarchy of human needs. Maslow presented the hierarchy in his 1943 paper entitled, "A Theory of Human Motivation" in *Psychological Review*. The five-stage pyramid model goes from basic needs to psychological needs. At the top of the pyramid is self-fulfillment. Here is how we see our eight archetypes within the Maslow framework:

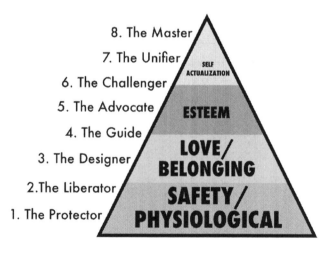

Let's now jump into the first of the eight archetypes: The Protector.

CHAPTER 7

THE PROTECTOR

*"The whole growth model we created over the last 50 years is
simply unsustainable economically and ecologically...
Both Mother Nature and Father Greed have hit the wall at once."*

—Thomas Friedman

The first archetype is The Protector. The purpose of The Protector is rooted in Maslow's concept of safety. The goal is to protect what is important.

Type: Safety

Category: Product

Archetype: The Protector - Those who protect what is important

Fiction: Superman, Captain John Miller (*Saving Private Ryan*)

Non-Fiction: Al Gore, Ralph Nader, Gloria Steinem

The symbol of The Protector is Superman. Brands with The Protector archetype are motivated to help others and their surroundings. In the words of the Man of Steel, "The welfare of Earth and all its people will always be my primary concern. But if there is a solution for hunger, it must be one that comes from the compassionate heart of man and extends outward toward his fellow man. To reach out to those in need and inspire others to do the same. That is life's greatest necessity and its most precious gift."

The Protector archetype can be broken down into the following sub-categories:

• Greenwashing: Campbell's

• General good unrelated to the business model: SC Johnson

- Responsible manufacturing: Numi Organic Tea

- Adding general good to an existing business model: Ben & Jerry's, Burt's Bee's, New Belgium

- Adding specific good directly related to the product to an existing business model: Cotopaxi

- Building product and purpose in tandem: Namaste Solar

- Starting with a desire to protect and build a product completely dedicated to its purpose: New Resource Bank

Let's look at 10 brands that have embraced the Protector archetype. To see more examples of this archetype, be sure to visit the Red Goldfish online resource library. There you'll find hundreds of great examples, training videos, and more case studies. Go to 602communications.com/redgoldfish

SUBCATEGORY: GREENWASHING

We've found that greenwashing happens most often at very large companies. Wall Street tends to focus on quick profits and quarterly returns. The result is that any sort of purpose-driven initiative is often seen as an indulgent distraction from the bottom line. In a world focused on quarterly returns, big companies have a hard time adding elements of purpose to their brand. Typically, successful purpose-driven brands tend to be ones that began small. Their business purpose was a founding principle and baked right into the company's culture. Over the years, that purpose was honed, defined, and implemented into a daily routine. Building a business model based on Milton Friedman's "profit-first" mindset and then turning that business toward purpose is hard to do. The types of purpose that greenwashing companies tend to pick can sometimes be just a bunch of noise.

Still, we don't want to criticize these companies that are making a genuine attempt to inject purpose into their business operations. Although greenwashing is not ideal, it's still a start. It can lead to bigger and better things. It's a first step for a company ready to consider that their business can be about more than just a quarterly return to investors.

1. CAMPBELL'S SOUP COMPANY PURPOSE STATEMENT

To promote global nutrition while building a sustainable environment that nourishes people's lives

Backstory: In 1869, Abraham Anderson, an icebox manufacturer, and Joseph Campbell, a fruit merchant, decided to join forces. The two Jersey boys produced canned tomatoes, vegetables, jellies, soups, condiments, and minced meats. Anderson left seven years later and eventually the business was named Joseph Campbell & Co. In 1897, an employee named John T. Dorrance developed a commercially viable method for condensing soup by halving the quantity of its heaviest ingredient: water. He went on to become president of the company from 1914 to 1930, eventually buying out the Campbell family.

CAMPBELL'S RED GOLDFISH: ACRE

Campbell's made a $125 million capital commitment to Acre Venture Partners, a Delaware-based limited partnership formed to make venture capital investments in "innovative new companies in food and food-related industries." Campbell's dedicated this fund to defining new approaches, business models, and smart external developments and to creating an ecosystem of innovative partners. The investment into Acre is a one of Campbell's recent moves aimed at becoming a more health-conscious company. For example, the company will be eliminating all artificial coloring and flavors from its North American portfolio by the end of fiscal 2018 and moving away from the use of high fructose corn syrup in certain products by the end of fiscal 2017. These actions taken by Campbell's point to their purpose "to promote global nutrition while building a sustainable environment that nourishes people's lives."

SUBCATEGORY: GENERAL GOOD UNRELATED TO THE BUSINESS MODEL

Companies that do general good unrelated to their offerings often times want to check the box. They realize that it is important to be a company that is a responsible community citizen. They create ways to bring their purpose to life without making it an intrinsic part of their business.

This is often handled by giving to charity or to unrelated causes. They will give to a foundation, or they will be eco-friendly under the guise of protection. These are oftentimes very heartfelt things, but these are companies that typically have not stepped into the power of building a product that can clearly demonstrate a purpose. This is a start to a good purpose-driven model. It introduces the idea of community good, which will then soften the ground down the road for something that can be purpose driven. Brands that take a general good strategy typically will treat purpose as a sideline because it is not something that makes them money, motivates employees, or has much to do with all of their activities on a daily basis. It will almost always be a sideline, and that could be a problem as business evolves.

2. SC JOHNSON PURPOSE STATEMENT

To promote global well-being.

Backstory: In 1886, Samuel Curtis Johnson, Sr. purchased the parquet flooring business of Racine Hardware Company. He renamed it Johnson's Prepared Paste Wax Company. Management of the private company has since passed down through five generations of the Johnson family. Today the company is known as SC Johnson & Son.

SC JOHNSON RED GOLDFISH: GREENLIST

After a decade of voluntarily removing chemicals from products, SC Johnson formally launched Greenlist in 2001. The goal was to go beyond taking out "bad" ingredients and instead focus on choosing "better" options and continuously improving formulas based on information about ingredients' impact on the environment and human health. Their goal is to increase the percentage of product ingredients that have a lower negative impact on the environment and human health. According to the company, their better/best ratio was 18% best in 2001. Today, in 2017, they report they are at 51% best. Greenlist initiatives have eliminated over 460 million pounds of manufacturing waste and removed more than 13.7 million pounds of volatile organic compounds from SC Johnson products. Going forward, the company plans to continue to "promote global wellbeing" by supporting cultural, educational, and public health projects that improve stakeholders' quality of life and by removing all toxicity and non-biodegradability from its household cleaning products. That is a direction toward fulfilling their purpose: to promote global well-being[12].

SUBCATEGORY: RESPONSIBLE MANUFACTURING

These are companies that produce a product and have done their best to try to bring a sense of morality and purpose to the way they

---

12. http://www.scjohnson.com/en/commitment/dialogue-on-sustainability/Business-with-a-Purpose.aspx

create that product. Typically, we've found these tend to be environmental brands that are making their product in sustainable ways. Groups that tend to be protected are the environment or employees. This category is all about being a responsible community citizen and taking care of all partners, including the environment, employees, partners, and investors. Everyone is seen as being able to win in this scenario. They want to make sure that they make maximum profit, but they want to do it so that it does not leave a trail of destruction behind them.

3. NUMI ORGANIC TEA PURPOSE STATEMENT

To create a healthful product that nurtures people and honors the planet

Backstory: After spending many years apart, one traveling the world and the other pursuing interests in art, brother and sister Ahmed and Reem Rahim met up during a family vacation at the the Grand Canyon. They began a discussion about starting a tea business. While living abroad, Ahmed had owned and operated teahouses in Europe. Reem had been studying art in Northern California. They wanted to create an entity that would encompass both of their passions. In 1999, after observing that competing brands in the US tea market differed little from one another in quality, consistency, and selection, Numi was created in a tiny 750 square foot apartment in Oakland, CA. Inspired by art and exotic teas, Reem and Ahmed created a company whose hallmark is super-premium, organic, and Fair Trade Certified teas and herbal teas made with 100% real ingredients[13].

---

13. http://greennaturemktg.com/product/numi-organic-tea/

NUMI RED GOLDFISH: NUMI CURRICULUM

The NUMI Curriculum brings nature, artistic expression, and social awareness to children in grades K-5. NUMI, in this context, stands for "Nature Underlies My Inspiration." It brings original and imaginative art and nature-based curriculums to children in inner city schools. The curriculums meet the Social Science and Language Arts content standards for California Public Schools and was developed based on the following principles:

Children learn to respect and have greater appreciation for their family, community, cultural heritage, and environment when they participate in a wide range of creative, multi-cultural, and educational experiences.

By nurturing creativity and imagination, children develop self-awareness, self-confidence, and the ability to visualize new possibilities.

When children are equipped with a bigger toolbox of creative skills combined with cultural and environmental understanding, they are more likely to grow into socially conscientious individuals who value and appreciate nature and their community.

A community that is served by socially conscious individuals will benefit and thrive in a globally healthy way.

The Numi Curriculum promotes respect for family, society, and the environment by raising cultural awareness and creativity in children. Combining this with their super-premium, organic product allows NUMI Organic Tea to live its purpose: to create a healthful product that nurtures people and honors the planet[14].

---

14. http://numifoundation.org/programs/numi-curriculum/

SUBCATEGORY: ADDING GENERAL GOOD TO AN EXISTING BUSINESS MODEL

Typically, these are established companies that have now decided it is time to inject a purpose into their businesses. This is a good strategy and typically is the next step up from the categories above. These are companies that often have a mismatch between what their product is and what their "good" is; however, they have built this idea of doing good into their entire business model, and therefore "good" has a much greater chance of success. The companies are firmly committed to doing good in the world. While the things that they do may be somewhat unrelated to their product, that spirit of doing good is still within the company's architecture, and they have created something that has the opportunity to become much more specific and much more integrated into the entire culture. Companies in this category may have begun by greenwashing, then started doing general good, and now have progressed far enough that they can recruit employees, community partners, and customers around their shared mission. The problem can be that the purpose is a little general. It's very hard to figure out a higher purpose for ice cream. It is tremendously tough to find a transcendent mission for beer. This can lead to a somewhat fuzzy purpose. They have done a really good job of being good people and of trying to build a company that is sustainable and great, but they have not fully developed a purpose-driven mission that their product can wholeheartedly support.

4. BEN & JERRY'S PURPOSE STATEMENT

To operate the company in a way that actively recognizes the central role that business plays in society by initiating innovative ways to improve the quality of life locally, nationally, and internationally.

Backstory: In 1978, good friends Ben Cohen and Jerry Greenfield decided to start a business together. They briefly considered bagels, but found the equipment was too expensive. Instead, they opted for to open a shop in Burlington, Vermont, featuring homemade ice cream. Armed with a five-dollar correspondence course about ice cream-making from Penn State, they turned an old gas station into a store. On their first anniversary, the store gave away free ice cream cones to thank the customers of their new business. They continue the practice today at Ben & Jerry's Homemade Ice Cream stores. Ben and Jerry were pioneers in developing a socially conscious business. They were proponents of the idea that businesses need to protect the environment. Ben & Jerry's is an advocate for what they call Climate Justice. In their words:

It's Not Climate Change… It's Everything Change

We live in a world where the effects of climate change are increasingly real; from melting ice caps to rampant forest fires, it can no longer be denied that manmade carbon pollution is affecting our fragile planet. The scientific evidence is settled; global warming is real and already impacting people around the world. The question now is, "What are we doing about it?" Every passing year, we see changing patterns of precipitation, including more intense rainfall events around the world, dramatic changes in the arctic, changes in agricultural growing seasons, and rising sea levels and ocean acidification. Some of these changes in our climate will have dramatic ecological and social consequences. The cruel irony of climate change is that people in the developing world, who can least afford to adapt to climate change, will pay the steepest price for the 200 years of industrialization and pollution from the developed world. It truly is an issue of climate justice[15].

---

15. http://www.benjerry.com/values/issues-we-care-about/climate-justice

The company believes that steps must be taken to dramatically reduce global greenhouse gas emissions – and to do it in a way that equitably shares the burdens and risks of climate change among the nations of the world. There is no quick fix to solve climate change, but the company advocates for:

- Divesting from fossil fuels

- Increasing renewable energy sources

- Putting a price on carbon pollution

- Working with developing countries to invest in renewable energy[16]

BEN & JERRY'S RED GOLDFISH: CHUNKINATOR

The company has calculated its carbon footprint and is working to reduce it. They are working with suppliers to reduce methane emissions from farms. They are changing to a cleaner, greener freezer in the US, and they have built the Chunkinator at their Netherlands factory. The Chunkinator helps power the factory from ice cream bi-products. Ben & Jerry's aims to get to 100% clean energy at all of their US sites by 2020. Ben & Jerry's works to reduce their carbon footprint, installing the Chunkinator in The Netherlands, and working toward using 100% clean energy at all their US sites speaks to their purpose " to operate the company in a way that actively recognizes the central role that business plays in society by initiating innovative ways to improve the quality of life locally, nationally, and internationally."

---

16. http://www.benjerry.com/values/issues-we-care-about/climate-justice

5. NEW BELGIUM BREWING PURPOSE STATEMENT

To manifest our love and talent by crafting our customers' favorite brands and proving business can be a force for good.

Backstory: Jeff Lebesch traveled to Europe in the summer of 1988 and toured Belgium on his mountain bike. He returned home to Colorado changed by the experience. Three years later, in the basement of his house, the electrical engineer installed some brewing equipment. It was there that Jeff created his first two Belgian-style beers. The first was a brown dubbel named Abbey. The second was an amber called Fat Tire, in honor of the Colorado tradition of calling mountain bikes 'Fat Tires.' Jeff's wife Kim Jordan also got involved. She became New Belgium's first bottler, sales rep, distributor, marketer, and financial planner. By the summer of 1991, the duo was selling Abbey and Fat Tire at festivals on the weekends. Less than one year later, the pair quit their day jobs and moved production out of the basement. The New Belgium Brewing Company was born. Before the first bottle of beer was ever sold, Jeff and Kim defined a clear purpose for New Belgium. The pair hiked into Rocky Mountain National Park with jug of home brew in one hand and pen/pad in the other. Here's what they wrote:

> COMPANY CORE VALUES AND BELIEFS
>
> Remembering that we are incredibly lucky to create something fine that enhances people's lives while surpassing our consumers' expectations
>
> Producing world-class beers
>
> Promoting beer culture and the responsible enjoyment of beer
>
> Kindling social, environmental and cultural change as a business role model

Environmental stewardship: Honoring nature at every turn of the business

Cultivating potential through learning, high involvement culture, and the pursuit of opportunities

Balancing the myriad needs of the company, our coworkers and their families

Trusting each other and committing to authentic relationships and communications

Continuous, innovative quality and efficiency improvements

Having fun[17]

NEW BELGIUM RED GOLDFISH(S): STEWARDSHIP GRANT PROGRAM AND BEER SCOUTS

Through its Environmental Stewardship Grant program–aka the $1 per Barrel program–New Belgium donates $1 for every barrel of beer sold to non-profits and causes. The company focuses on a few big categories, one of which is bicycle advocacy and sensible transportation. In 2014, New Belgium gave $105,000 to support local organizations around the country that are working to make the bike a viable form of transportation in their communities[18].

Beer Scouts is an interdepartmental group from New Belgian Brewing. The group sponsors volunteer events for coworkers and community members as a means to give back and inspire positive change. They formed their group with the goal of connecting busy people to projects they might be passionate about that are aligned

17. http://www.newbelgium.com/Brewery/company/history
18. http://www.newbelgium.com/Sustainability/Stories/new-belgium-brewing/2014/11/10/A-Buck-a-Barrel-for-More-Bikes-Boom

with New Belgium's values. Beer Scouts have helped log 12,500 volunteer hours of coworker time in the past five years; 2,773 of those volunteer hours were logged in 2015. New Belgium appreciates employee volunteers with paid time off for their efforts. Employees receive one hour of PTO for every two hours of volunteer work. While New Belgian has not posted a company "purpose," the company's actions respectably live out a number of aspects in their list of core values and beliefs[19].

6. BURT'S BEES PURPOSE STATEMENT

To protect and harness the power of nature to help your skin work beautifully

Backstory: Burt Shavitz was a passionate beekeeper, wisecracker, and lover of nature from Maine. His business started out simply. He focused on doing what he loved—making honey from beehives. Eventually, the leftover beeswax was turned into candles. Later on, it was used for lip balm and other products under the name of Burt's Bees.

BURT'S BEES RED GOLDFISH: BEE BUFFER PROJECT

Burt's Bees, through its The Greater Good Foundation, established the Bee Buffer Project to create critical pollinator forage throughout the country. Burt's will impact over 20,000 acres as part of their long-term plans. Bees rely on land and flora for a variety of nutrients to survive and prevent disease, just like humans. And bees pollinate one third of all food we eat. They are crucial to both human and environmental health, impacting biodiversity, food security, nutrition and sustainable land use. Since 2007, Burt's Bees has supported honeybee health initiatives and research. The work carried

---

19. http://www.newbelgium.com/Sustainability/Community/BeerScouts

out by the Bee Buffer Project has a positive impact on both our environment and our health by protecting our pollinators, which does direct itself toward the company's "protect and harness the power of nature" purpose as it creates skin care products.

SUBCATEGORY: ADDING SPECIFIC GOOD DIRECTLY RELATED TO THE EXISTING BUSINESS MODEL

These are typically companies that have been in business awhile and have a firm business model going and then decide that they want to find something with purpose that they can stand for that is directly related to the product. Typically the purpose they define adds value in a way that directly relates back to the daily operation of the business and supports the company's current product-focused priorities. This is a great way to bring purpose to something that the company already does well and to maintain profit and infrastructure that currently exist in the company while adding good.

7. COTOPAXI PURPOSE STATEMENT

To inspire social and environmental change that results in the improvement of the human condition and the amelioration of poverty

Backstory: Wharton graduate Davis Smith created an outdoor gear company with a humanitarian mission. He named the company Cotopaxi after the volcano that looms over Quito, the capital of Ecuador. His original business model was similar to Toms Shoes and Warby Parker. Currently, two percent of Cotopaxi's sales is earmarked to help nonprofits focused on education, health, and livelihood. They are committed to making an impact with their work to reduce global poverty by their active collaboration with organizations to build sustainable solutions for local communities.

COTOPAXI RED GOLDFISH: QUESTIVALS

Cotopaxi stages one-day adventure races it called Questivals, in which teams of two to six people complete outdoor challenges for a chance to win gear and trips. At the company's World Championship, participants will race across seven countries from Belize to Panama. Along the way, they'll have to squeeze in good work, such as volunteering in soup kitchens. Armchair adventurers can track the progress of the teams on a proprietary app. Questivals provide a very specific connection to the outdoor gear-adventure direction of the company's products while it adds the doing good element of social change and poverty relief that speaks strongly to the company's purpose "to inspire social and environmental change that results in the improvement of the human condition and the amelioration of poverty."[20]

SUBCATEGORY: BUILDING A PRODUCT AND PURPOSE IN TANDEM

These are companies that have built a product and a purpose side-by-side. They typically are smaller companies that have a tendency to create something that has a specific mission behind it. These are very successful brands and do a great job of building a purpose and a product side-by-side.

8. NAMASTE SOLAR PURPOSE STATEMENT

To propagate the responsible use of solar energy and pioneer conscientious business practices

Backstory: Blake Jones, Ray Tuomey, and Wes Kennedy turned to the Sanskrit word Namasté for their solar panel company in 2005. The Sanskrit word has important meaning as a traditional greeting

---

20. http://www.bloomberg.com/news/articles/2016-04-21/cotopaxi-stitches-social-goals-into-every-backpack

of respect. The word recognizes the interdependence of all living things. They chose this word because it represents their company values well and because they felt it had a unique ability to differentiate their company from other solar companies.

NAMASTE RED GOLDFISH: 10%

Namaste's Red Goldfish is very simple. They donate 10% of their annual profits to their community in the form of:

- In-kind donations

- Sponsorships

- Volunteer days

- Contributions

This Red Goldfish may not tie directly to the company's product or appear to tie in directly with the company's purpose at first glance. It does, however, live out the company culture expressed by their name as the company is an integral part of doing good within their community.

SUBCATEGORY: PROTECTING THINGS IMPORTANT TO CUSTOMERS BUT NOT INTRINSIC TO THE BUSINESS

These companies talk to customers and find out the things that are most important to them. They then inject those customer values into their own businesses. For example, Timberland is about environmentalism. There is nothing intrinsically environmental about a sweater or pair of shoes. However, people who tend to buy outdoor gear also tend to want to protect the planet. These companies have a loose connection of their purpose to their product, but they have an incredibly specific connection to their customer base.

9. PATAGONIA PURPOSE STATEMENT

To help reimagine a sustainable world for those who come after us.

Backstory: Yvon Chouinard got his start as a climber in 1953 as a 14-year-old member of the Southern California Falconry Club when one of the adult leaders, Don Prentice, taught Yvon how to rappel down the cliffs to the falcon aeries. The only pitons available at that time were made of soft iron, placed once, then left in the rock. After meeting John Salathé, a Swiss climber who had once made hard-iron pitons out of Model A axles, Chouinard decided to make his own reusable hardware. In 1957, he went to a junkyard and bought a used coal-fired forge, a 138-pound anvil, some tongs and hammers, and started teaching himself how to blacksmith. The word spread and soon friends were asking for Chouinard's chrome-molybdenum steel pitons. Before he knew it, he was in business. He could forge two of his pitons in an hour, and he sold them for $1.50 each. By 1970, Chouinard Equipment had become the largest supplier of climbing hardware in the US. That year, on a winter climbing trip to Scotland, Chouinard bought a regulation team rugby shirt to wear rock climbing. Overbuilt to withstand the rigors of rugby, it had a collar that would keep the hardware slings from cutting into the neck. It was blue with two red and one yellow center stripe across the chest. Back in the States, Yvon wore it around his climbing friends. They asked where they could get one. Before long, Chouinard saw clothing as a way to help support the marginally profitable hardware business. As his company made more and more clothes, they needed to find a name for their clothing line. According to Yvon, "To most people, especially then, Patagonia was a name like Timbuktu or Shangri-La, far-off, interesting, not quite on the map. Patagonia brings to mind, as we once wrote in a catalog introduction, 'romantic visions of glaciers tumbling into fjords, jagged windswept peaks, gauchos, and condors.' It's been a good name for us, and it can be pronounced in every language."

PATAGONIA RED GOLDFISH: GREEN SABBATICALS

One popular Patagonia perk is a program that allows employees to take off up to two months at full pay to do work for environmental groups. In one green sabbatical, Lisa Myers, who works on the company's giving programs, tracked wolves in Yellowstone National Park. "It's easy to go to work when you get paid to do what you love to do," says Myers. Green sabbaticals are clearly about protecting the world for those who come after us and will connect very directly to the people who are in tune with Patagonia products and have a passion for enjoying and protecting our world[21].

SUBCATEGORY: STARTING WITH A DESIRE TO PROTECT AND BUILD A PRODUCT COMPLETELY DEDICATED TO THE COMMITMENT

These are the most successful brands in the protection category. Where a founder typically began a process that created a product out of a problem. The company found some indiscretion in the world, they saw a problem that bothered them, and they sought to make a difference.

10. NEW RESOURCE BANK PURPOSE STATEMENT

To achieve well-being for all people and the planet through banking

Backstory: New Resource Bank was founded in 2006 with a vision of bringing new resources to sustainable businesses and ultimately creating more-sustainable communities. The San Francisco, California-based bank wants to advance sustainability on every level: the loans it makes, its own operations, and its engagement with the community. In 2010, New Resource became a B Corporation. The bank's goal is a loan portfolio with 100 percent invested in busi-

---

21. http://www.bloomberg.com/news/articles/2006-08-20/a-passion-for-the-planet

nesses that are advancing sustainability. All new loan recipients must be green businesses or committed to improving their operational sustainability and managing their impact on society and the environment. It has become a purpose driven lender in the areas of clean tech, "green" products, eco real estate, and any other businesses run on clear sustainability principles.

NEW RESOURCE BANK RED GOLDFISH: RE:THINK EVENTS

New Resource holds free workshops and networking events. They are designed to foster community, encourage dialogue, and delve deep into sustainability themes.

Visit our website to see great video examples from each of these companies and many more Protector archetype businesses. Go to 602communications.com/redgoldfish

The next archetype is The Liberator.

CHAPTER 8

THE LIBERATOR

"I've always believed that when you spend so much of your life working, you should do everything you can to make it fun. It should be something you can be passionate about and care deeply about."

— Richard Branson

The second archetype is The Liberator. The purpose of The Liberator is rooted in Maslow's concept of safety. The goal is to liberate and help others by reinventing a broken system and striving to help others break away from bondage.

Type: Safety

Category: Product

Archetype: The Liberator - Reinvent a broken system

Fiction: Jason Bourne

Non-Fiction: Che Guevara, Richard Branson, Henry Ford, Margaret Thatcher, Moses

The symbol of The Liberator is Moses. Brands with The Liberator archetype are motivated to do things differently, leading others to a better place. In the words of Moses, "All who thirst for freedom may come with us. Tomorrow the light of freedom will shine upon us as we go forth from Egypt."

The entire category can be divided into two main groups:

Stakeholder Liberators – advocates with a focus on improving the situation for customers, vendors, stockholders, and employees. Here are the types:

•   Shaking off an oppressor: Harley Davidson

•   Liberate employees: SAS

•   Liberate customers: Jordan's Furniture, Southwest Airlines

Business Practice Liberators – companies with a focus on better business practices. They seek to improve innovation, workflow, process, and business operations. Here are the types:

- Workflow liberators: Good Eggs

- Manufacturing liberators: Honest Tea, IKEA

- Technology liberators: airBNB

- Product feature liberators: Sungevity, Netflix

Let's look at 11 brands that have embraced The Liberator archetype. To see more examples of this archetype, visit the Red Goldfish on-line resource library. There you'll find hundreds of great examples, training videos and more case studies. Go to 602communications. com/redgoldfish

We'll start with the stakeholder liberators.

SUBCATEGORY: STAKEHOLDER LIBERATORS

Shaking off an oppressor.

These companies most often position themselves as rebels who are standing up for the simple man who is being somehow oppressed by the large and uncaring legacy players in the sector. They position customers as martyrs who have had to put up with uncaring, profit-mongering, exploitative, money-hungry, abusive category leaders. Virgin embodies this approach. The company moves into existing sectors, straps on the cross, then positions itself as leading everyday people to the promised land. They've done this in many different sectors. It began with the record industry, where they provided a new shopping experience for a better way to buy music. They have done it with the airline industry by positioning British Airways as a government-run monopoly that was exploiting people. They did it in the telecom industry, positioning existing telecommunications companies as overpriced with terrible service. Virgin offered flexible plans and low-cost alternatives to the big expensive players. Harley-Davidson rebels against everything. They see the entire world as an oppressor, but particularly those in authority. Harley riders see themselves as outlaws who do not follow the rules. Any rule that has been made is meant to be broken by a Harley-Davidson rider.

1. HARLEY DAVIDSON PURPOSE STATEMENT

To fulfill dreams of personal freedom through the experience of motorcycling.

Backstory: In 1901, William S. Harley completed a blueprint drawing of an engine designed to fit onto a bicycle. Two years later, Harley partnered with Arthur Davidson to make the first production Harley-Davidson motorcycle available to the public. The bike was built to be a racer. It had a 3-1/8 inch bore and 3-1/2 inch stroke. The factory in which they worked was a 10 x 15-foot wooden shed with the words "Harley-Davidson Motor Company" crudely scrawled on the door. On July 4th, 1905, a Harley-Davidson motorcycle won a 15-mile race in Chicago with a time of 19:02. That same year in Milwaukee, their first full-time employee was hired[22].

RED GOLDFISH: FREE RIDING ACADEMY CLASSES

Harley offers free riding academy classes. In 2016, it offered free Riding Academy motorcycle classes for first responders, including firefighters, police, and emergency medical service personnel. The announcement came on the heels of a year-long extension of free

---

22. https://www.harley-davidson.com/content/h-d/en_US/home/museum/explore/hd-history/1900.html

rider training for all current and former members of the US military. Harley's free rider training to military personnel and first responders not only fulfills the "dreams of personal freedom through the experience of motorcycling" of its purpose but also gains appreciation from a broad range of its customers who also value the dedication and sacrifices made by first responders and our military personnel.

EMPLOYEE LIBERATORS

These are companies that pride themselves on the humane and nurturing ways they treat their own employees. They offer optimal benefits, normal hours, work-life balance, and motivation around a mission. Oftentimes, these are companies firmly grounded in their purpose. Caring for employee groups allows them to recruit better people, reduce turnover, and build a strong organization based on an individual purpose. These companies vary in their focus. On one side are the very general employee benefit missions that include many different things such as pay, vacation, daycare, cafeterias, training, and meaningful work. On the other side of this continuum are companies with a very specific employee missions centered around far fewer benefits. These companies typically have a purpose such as environmentalism, compassion, feminism, etc. The benefit here is not so much wrapped up in a general package of general benefits but rather is firmly grounded in a passionate mission for constituency.

2. SAS PURPOSE STATEMENT

To help customers make better decisions faster.

Backstory: In 1967, a graduate student named James Goodnight joined a project at North Carolina State University to create a statistical analysis system (SAS) for university agricultural departments. It became an independent, private business led by current CEO James Goodnight and three other project leaders from the university in 1976. The company invested in innovation and employee retention. SAS' workplace environment and benefits program is designed to retain employees. It provides on-site, subsidized or free healthcare, gyms, daycare, and counseling services. Today, the company is the largest privately held software company in the world. SAS sets the bar high for its employees and then provides a culture that fosters creativity and promotes innovation. This approach springs from Goodnight's philosophy: "Treat employees like they make a difference and they will." SAS has been recognized for its workplace culture by various organizations, including the Great Place to Work®[23].

RED GOLDFISH: SAS REWARDS

SAS Rewards describes the investments the company makes in employee health, well-being, and work-life balance. The benefit to SAS is a dedicated workforce, a group committed to moving up the ranks rather than out the door. Their turnover rate of about 4 percent is far below the industry average of 15 percent, which translates into consistent, long-term relationships for customers. By taking care of their employees, the rest takes care of itself[24].

CUSTOMER LIBERATORS

This category is very similar to "shaking off an oppressor," but the focus is not on another company as a villain but on the specific circumstances the constituents must endure in their purchasing process. Typically, there is some onerous process that the customer must endure. The liberator company vociferously points out the

---

23. http://www.sas.com/en_us/company-information/great-workplace.html
24. http://www.sas.com/en_us/careers/life-at-sas.html#benefits

shortcomings professing "this is just not right." Then, with some sort of innovation, the company eliminates the major problem, providing a refreshing, rejuvenative experience that makes the process positive again. Most all these companies also would qualify for a "business practice liberator" tag as well, but here the focus is not so much on the process surrounding the liberation, but on the customer's experience of the oppression and the positive feelings that come from relieving that oppression.

3. JORDAN'S FURNITURE PURPOSE STATEMENT

To allow the average person to be able to afford high quality furniture.

Backstory: Jordan's Furniture was started by Samuel Tatelman in 1918 in Waltham, Massachusetts. Samuel sold furniture out of the back of a truck until 1926. In the late 1930s, his son Edward joined the business. In 1973, Barry and Eliot Tatelman took over the business from their father, Edward. In 1983, Barry and Eliot built and opened the Nashua, New Hampshire, facility. In 1987, they opened the Avon, Massachusetts, facility and created the largest traffic jam ever recorded on Route 24. Barry and Eliot had to go on the radio to beg people not to come. Customers stood in line for hours waiting for their turn to go into the showroom. There are currently seven Jordan's Furniture locations: Reading, Avon, Taunton, Natick, Nashua, Warwick, and New Haven.

RED GOLDFISH: UNDERPRICE GUARANTEE

Buying furniture or a mattress at the right price shouldn't be difficult. Jordan's Furniture guarantees it won't be. For over 90 years, Jordan's has been committed to providing the largest selection of quality furniture and mattresses at the very best prices. Here is their guarantee:

"If you find a lower advertised price on identical merchandise under the same terms and conditions from another store-based retailer within the local Retail Trade Area within 30 days of purchase, Jordan's Furniture will refund the difference. The Underprice Guarantee enables you to buy in confidence, knowing you will be getting the best price everyday." So the Red Goldfish with Jordan is as basic yet significant as removing the hassle consumers experience buying mattresses or new furniture–a welcome relief for the buyer–connecting with the company's purpose achieved by providing affordable, high quality products[25].

4. SOUTHWEST AIRLINES PURPOSE STATEMENT

To connect people to what's important in their lives through friendly, reliable, and low-cost air travel.

Backstory: More than 38 years ago, Rollin King and Herb Kelleher got together and decided to start a different kind of airline. They began with one simple notion: If you get your passengers to their destinations when they want to get there, on time, at the lowest possible fares, and make darn sure they have a good time doing it, people will fly your airline. On June 18, 1971, the love airline was born. Dallas, San Antonio, and Houston were their initial three cities. The airline offered $20 one-way fares. Captain Emilio Salazar piloted the inaugural flight[26].

RED GOLDFISH: BAGS FLY FREE

Southwest Airlines does not charge for your first or second checked bag. While bag fees have become the norm among their competitors, Southwest has stayed true to its reputation as the maverick of the airline industry by not charging for bags. Lagniappe: skis and

---

25. http://www.jordans.com/customer-service/retail-and-delivery-policies/underprice-guarantee
26. https://www.southwest.com/html/about-southwest/index.html?int

golf bags fly free as well. Passengers save up to $120 round trip with Bags Fly Free. With the challenges of air travel bedeviling travelers, Southwest endears itself to its customers with the "gift" of bags traveling for free. Including things like skis and golf bags in Bags Fly Free further liberates people to connect with "what's important in their lives through friendly, reliable, and low-cost air travel."

5. CARMAX PURPOSE STATEMENT

To liberate the car buying experience by offering great quality cars, at no haggle prices, with exceptional customer service.

Backstory: The concept for CarMax was developed by Circuit City executives under former CEO Richard L. Sharp. It was developed for nearly a year during 1991 using the codename "Project X." It was also known as "Honest Rick's Used Cars" to those intimately involved in the skunk works team. The concept was actually first proposed by a consultant hired by Circuit City to evaluate possible business opportunities beyond the scope of their consumer electronics locations. The first CarMax location opened in September 1993.

RED GOLDFISH: TRANSPARENT PRICING

CarMax broke away from traditional car selling. They changed how buyers purchase cars. CarMax appraises the customer's car and offers to buy it from them at the store with a transparent offer. The offer doesn't change whether you buy a car from CarMax or not. If you purchase, there is complete transparency and no haggle pricing. CarMax has sold over six million cars, all at the price that's stickered on that car – the CarMax car price is posted on every vehicle they sell. CarMax sales associates are commissioned, but they make the same commission off a $5,000 car that they make on a $15,000 car. There is no individual incentive to upsell. The sales associate's job is to work with the consumer to put them in the car that's right for them. Plus, if the car is not what the consumer needs, it can be brought back within five days. It allows for alignment between the selling process and the consumer's best interest. CarMax's transparent pricing is a Red Goldfish that liberates customers from car-buying price-haggling drama, fulfilling a significant portion of its purpose.

SUBCATEGORY: BUSINESS PRACTICE LIBERATORS

WORKFLOW LIBERATORS

These businesses have somehow managed to change and optimize the workflow in established categories to improve the customer experience. This is handled in some fairly typical ways.

Cutting out the middleman: Many of these businesses provide direct services to consumers cutting out middlemen to reduce weight, cost, and gain efficiency. These businesses are typified by companies such as Good Eggs and Amazon. Increasing efficiency and cutting out red tape: These companies streamline the business process optimize the customer experience. Other workflow liberators focus on eliminating exploitive practices. These companies are close to the "shaking off an oppressor" category, but their focus is on the business instead of persecution. Marquee Lawyers, for example, does not operate on an hourly basis, thus saving its clients money and making them project-based which increases efficiency.

6. GOOD EGGS PURPOSE STATEMENT

To connect people who love food directly with people who make it.

Backstory: Good Eggs was founded in San Francisco in 2011 with a mission to grow and sustain local food systems worldwide. The company now works with hundreds of local and sustainable food producers and delivers delicious, fresh food seven days a week across the San Francisco Bay Area. With its innovative model, the company operates a foodhub where orders are prepped and packed, but products aren't stored for more than a few hours. Customers place their orders in advance and producers deliver exactly what's been purchased. Food is made fresh, delivered to Good Eggs, and then delivered to the customer all in the same day… just in time for dinner. Good Eggs culture holds the ideal that we all are responsible for helping to create a better world[27].

RED GOLDFISH: STANDARDS

Good Eggs believes in a food system where small local businesses are connected directly with customers in their community. They work with high-integrity, national brands when local sourcing isn't possible or feasible. They think the best tasting food is made by people who care. They taste every product, vet every business, and make sure that every brand they work with—big or small—is held to their rigorous criteria:

- People - Good Eggs food producers pay their employees a fair wage. Good Eggs maintains a direct relationship with every food producer in their marketplace. Each producer gives back to their communities in tangible ways.

- Planet - Customers can pronounce and understand all of the ingredients in the products. Any animal products used are raised without growth hormones. Farmers are guided by principles of sustainability.

- Transparency - Food producers have a deep knowledge of their own supply chains and can trace all of their ingredients back to

---

27. https://www.bcorporation.net/community/good-eggs

their sources. Food producers are happy to answer questions about their practices and welcome visits to their farms.

Good Eggs' commitment to their standards of local sourcing, high quality product standards, and fair wages is an appealing Red Goldfish to their employees, producers, and customers.

MANUFACTURING LIBERATORS

While workflow liberators concentrate on business practices, manufacturing operators are firmly focused on a better product. This could mean a specific individual feature that is baked into the product, such as an organic coffee or real tea revolutionizing how a drink is made to quench thirst. It could also be focused on a manufacturing process. Birkenstock prides itself on never bowing to fashion and creating the ultimate "footbed" in shoes that provide ultimate comfort. It manufactures shoes in an entirely unique way, and it wears that on its sleeve and feet. It could also be about manufacturing efficiency, the ability to create the same product for less money, such as IKEA making furniture and packaging it in revolutionary ways.

7. HONEST TEA PURPOSE STATEMENT

To promote sustainability and great taste in organic beverages.

Backstory: Seth Goldman, co-founder of Honest Tea, drank a lot of liquids. An active person, Seth was continually in search of the perfect drink to quench his thirst after a run, a game of basketball, or between grad school classes. Yet, Seth found most drinks either too sweet or too tasteless. Barry Nalebuff, Seth's professor at the Yale School of Management, found that he and Seth shared a passion for the idea of a less sweet, but flavorful beverage during a class discussion of a Coke vs. Pepsi case study. They agreed that there were tons of sweet options and lots of watery drinks, but in 1994, there was nothing in between to fill the void. Fast forward to 1997. Seth went for a run in New York City with a college friend who used to concoct juice drinks with him after class. As they found themselves doing the same beverage mixing after the run, Seth knew then that if he was going to quench his thirst for good, he would have to create the drink himself. He later e-mailed Barry to see if he was excited about the idea. Timing was everything. Barry had just returned from India where he had been analyzing the tea industry for a case study. Barry had even come up with a name to describe a bottled tea that was made with real tea leaves–Honest Tea. When Seth heard the name, the simmering idea began to boil–it was the perfect name for a brand that would strive to create honest relationships with its customers, suppliers, and the environment. Seth took a deep breath, quit his job at Calvert Mutual Funds and started brewing batches of tea in his kitchen. Five weeks after taking the plunge, he brought thermoses of tea and a recycled bottle with a mock-up label to Fresh Fields (Whole Foods Market). The buyer ordered 15,000 bottles, and Seth and Barry were in business–if they could figure out how to make that much tea. They did[28].

RED GOLDFISH: GETTING FAIR WITH SUGAR

The organic cane sugar used in Honest Tea in glass bottles is Fair Trade Certified. The premiums from the purchase of Fair Trade Certified cane sugar make a difference for the farming communities. In Paraguay, a co-op of sugar farmers chose to invest in new farm equipment, healthcare, education, and a safety net for older workers. They are also finding alternatives to conventional pesticides, such as using wasps to control cane worms[29]. Honest Tea built a better product for those who wanted a flavorful drink beyond sweet beverages or water beverages. By incorporating Fair

28. https://www.honesttea.com/about-us/our-story/
29. https://www.honesttea.com/blog/why-keep-it-honest/

Trade Certified cane sugar, Honest Tea's Red Goldfish product fulfills the company's purpose to promote sustainability and great taste in organic beverages.

8. IKEA PURPOSE STATEMENT

To create a better everyday life for the many people

Backstory: Ingvar Feodor Kamprad was born on the 30th of March, 1926, on a small farm called Elmtaryd near the rural village of Agunnaryd in the Swedish province of Småland. Kamprad began his career at the age of six, selling matches. When he was ten, he crisscrossed the neighborhood on his bicycle selling Christmas decorations, fish, and pencils. At 17, in 1943, Kamprad's father rewarded him with a small sum of money for doing well in school despite being dyslexic. With the money, Ingvar founded a business named IKEA, an abbreviation for Ingvar Kamprad from Elmtaryd, Agunnaryd, his boyhood home. Two years after starting IKEA, Kamprad began using milk trucks to deliver his goods. In 1947, he started selling furniture made by local manufacturers. By 1955, manufacturers began boycotting IKEA, protesting against Kamprad's low prices. This forced him to design items in-house. The basic IKEA concept–simple, affordable furniture, designed, distributed and sold in-house–was complete. IKEA believed that anyone should be able to afford stylish, modernist furniture. Kamprad felt he was not just cutting costs and making money but was serving the people as well. Today, IKEA is on the path to becoming the world's largest furniture retailer. The IKEA catalogue is distributed twice a widely as the Bible.

RED GOLDFISH: FLAT PACK

In 1953, Gilles Lundgren joined IKEA as a catalog manager. Three years later, he was tasked with delivering a new, leaf-shaped table called the Lovet to a nearby photo studio so it could be shot for an upcoming catalog. But he got frustrated trying to fit the table into his small post-war car. "When I looked at how we might keep a large number of these tables at our low price," he once said, "I thought: 'Why not take off the legs?'" The rest was history. Lundgren never claimed he was the inventor of flat-pack furniture. A fellow Swede, Fiolke Ohlsson, patented a ready-to-assemble chair in 1949. Lundgren's legacy was in popularizing flat-pack. He became such a tireless advocate for flat-pack furniture that he soon convinced Kamprad to make it the cornerstone of the fledgling furniture maker's business model. As simple but innovative as designing and making furniture that is able to be packed flat for shipping and then easily assembled is a Red Goldfish for transport and customers alike[30].

TECHNOLOGY LIBERATORS

These are companies that have harnessed technology to create a better customer experience. Typically, this is Internet technology that allows for optimal customization, decreased cost, and direct manufacturer interaction. Dyson does not use Internet technology but positions itself as a master of vacuum cleaner technology. They are engineers and wear that badge proudly.

9. AIRBNB PURPOSE STATEMENT

To open up the world, a world where people belong, anywhere.

Backstory: In October of 2007, Brian Chesky and Joe Gebbia were living in a San Francisco apartment. They couldn't afford rent. That weekend, an international design conference was coming to town, and all of the hotels were sold out. The pair had an idea. In Chesky's words, "Why not turn our place into a bed and breakfast for the

---

30. https://www.fastcodesign.com/3057837/the-man-behind-ikeas-world-conquering-flat-pack-design

conference?" They inflated airbeds and called it the AirBed & Breakfast. From that first airbed, airBNB grew person-to-person, block-by-block, city-by-city. Today, the community is in 34,000 cities in 192 countries. This idea is about much more than just making ends meet. At airBNB, they are creating a door to an open world– where everyone's at home and can belong, anywhere.

RED GOLDFISH: AIRBNB DISASTER RESPONSE

airBNB's Disaster Response Program helps house disaster victims for free. The program was launched in 2012 after Hurricane Sandy struck. It was inspired by the 1,400 airBNB hosts who provided Sandy victims with meals and roofs over their heads in New York. airBNB decided to create an official tool that enables airBNB hosts around the world to help those in need during times of crisis. Through this tool, the Disaster Response Program connects those in need with airBNB hosts who have opened their doors to evacuees, providing safe places to stay in affected areas. airBNB's Nick Shapiro said, "We are hopeful that airBNB can help play a small part in making the evacuation process easier for residents and their families." airBNB Disaster Response Program exemplifies using technology to connect a world where people belong, anywhere, including when disaster has struck, by allowing the airBNB community to connect with those in need– whether it be business or pleasure accommodations or shelter after a calamity.

PRODUCT FEATURE LIBERATORS

These are companies that have chosen not to showcase their manufacturing, technology, or workflow but instead have lasered in on a very specific product feature that they feel is a deal breaker within the sector. This sector is halfway between a customer focus and a business practice focus. Typically, they have a single outstanding feature. The problem with these businesses is that once competitors catch up to that feature, their business model is in trouble.

10. SUNGEVITY PURPOSE STATEMENT

To improve the process of going solar.

Backstory: Danny Kennedy recognized that solar energy wasn't well understood by the public, the technology at hand wasn't efficient, and trying to put solar energy to use was, as he put it, "a hassle." He decided to do something about this. He wanted consumers to think about solar energy as a true alternative energy source, so he needed to change their attitudes about and experiences with solar energy use. In order to fulfill his mission to change attitudes about solar energy, Kennedy, Alec Guettel, a long time friend, and former banker Andrew Birch came together to found Sungevity. Their goal was to create a solution that would make solar energy an easy choice for homeowners. The large initial investment required to purchase the solar panels and the up front cost for panel installation was a stumbling block for many who might otherwise consider the switch from traditional energy to solar. Their reward for that outlay was only a promise of savings down the road. Sungevity came up with an innovative response to this hurdle. They offer their customers a "solar lease." Customers pay a monthly rate for their panels and save money on their electric bill from the time of installation. Sungevity not only eases the pain of the financial investment, the company walks homeowners through the process of going solar, step-by-step, starting with the quote and following through with the installation. They have taken something that was expensive, unwieldy, and not very efficient at any level, put a process to it, added useful technology, and made it easy to make the decision to move to solar energy[31].

---

31. http://www.huffingtonpost.com/2012/09/04/danny-kennedy-sungevity-solar_n_1853927.html

RED GOLDFISH: NON-PROFIT PARTNERSHIPS

Sungevity partners with non-profit organizations to engage their networks with powerful solar solutions while raising funds to support their valuable work. When those who support the non-profit go solar with Sungevity and use the non-profit's referral code, the supporter benefits from the use of solar energy, the non-profit they support benefits from an award from Sungevity, and the planet benefits. Specifically, when a non-profit's referral code is used for a new solar installation, Sungevity will send a check to the non-profit for a minimum of $750 within 90 days after that system is installed and connected to the grid. Sungevity has raised over $2 million for their non-profit partners, which helps support their critical work. When members of their networks make the switch to generating energy from sunshine, they can benefit themselves, their organization and the environment[32]. By focusing on doing good through the sale of a product, Sungevity has created a Red Goldfish that supports non-profit partners and benefits the new solar customer, all while protecting the earth.

11. NETFLIX PURPOSE STATEMENT

To promote the freedom of on-demand and the fun of indulgent viewing.

Backstory: Reed Hastings walked into Blockbuster in 1997 to return a movie. He walked out annoyed with having just paid a $40 late fee. In his words, "I remember the fee because I was embarrassed about it. That was back in the VHS days, and it got me thinking that there's a big market out there." Hastings had recently sold his first company, Pure Software, for $750 million. It wasn't the money that bothered Hastings. It was the inconvenience of having to deal with getting the video returned within the allotted time. Thinking there

---

32. http://sungevity.org

had to be a better way to rent videos, Hastings investigated the idea of creating a movie-rental business by mail. "I didn't know about DVDs, and then a friend of mine told me they were coming. I ran out to Tower Records in Santa Cruz and mailed CDs to myself, just a disc in an envelope. It was a long 24 hours until the mail arrived back at my house, and I ripped them open and they were all in great shape." The idea for Netflix was born[33].

Netflix has changed its delivery system over the years, but its core service remains the customer-centric delivery of on-demand entertainment.

RED GOLDFISH: NO-HASSLE CANCELLATION POLICY

Netflix has a no-hassle cancellation policy. According to Hastings, "We are counter-positioned against the hassles, complexity, and frustration that embodies most [services]. We strive to be extremely straightforward and simple. There is no better embodiment of this than our no-hassle online cancellation. Members can leave when they want and come back when they want[34]." The Red Goldfish is simple: stream your entertainment for a small fee, join or leave whenever you want—without frustrations or consequences—fulfilling the freedom of on-demand and the fun of indulgent viewing purpose of the company.

The next archetype is The Designer.

---

33. http://www.inc.com/magazine/20051201/qa-hastings.html

34. http://files.shareholder.com/downloads/NFLX/2441659654x0x656145/e4410bd8-e5d4-4d31-ad79-84c36c49f77c/IROverviewHomePageLetter_4.24.13_pdf.pdf

CHAPTER 9

THE DESIGNER

*"Technology is nothing. What's important is that you have
faith in people, that they're basically good and smart,
and if you give them tools, they'll do wonderful things with them."*

— Steve Jobs

The third archetype is The Designer. The purpose of The Designer is rooted in Maslow's concept of safety and love. The goal is to empower others through the creation of revolutionary products.

Type: Safety/Love

Category: Product

Archetype: The Designer - Empowering through revolutionary products

Fiction: Doc Brown, MacGyver, Willy Wonka

Non-Fiction: Steve Jobs, Thomas Edison, James Dyson, Leonardo DaVinci

The symbol of The Designer is Doc Brown. Brands with The Designer archetype are creators. They persist in building stylish products that change the world. They are wired to push through adversity. In the words of Doc Brown from *Back to the Future,* "The way I see it, if you're gonna build a time machine into a car, why not do it with some style?"

This archetype can be broken down into the follow subcategories:

- Functionality designers: Apple

- Artistic designers: Method Home, IDEO

- Product feature designers: Paper Culture, 3M

- Customer experience designers: Zappos, Disney

- High-Tech designers: Tesla

- Protecting designers: Tom Organics

Let's look at nine brands that have embraced The Designer archetype. To see more examples of this archetype, visit the Red Goldfish online resource library for hundreds of great examples, training videos, and more case studies. Go to 602communications.com/redgoldfish

SUBCATEGORY: FUNCTIONALITY DESIGNERS

These companies have brought an entirely new level of usability and functionality to their products. They make them more assessable, easier to use, and generate a delightful experience because of the efficiency of the interaction. Typically, these companies have found ways to cut waste, eliminate middlemen, and bring the customer closer to the experience of using the direct product.

1. APPLE PURPOSE STATEMENT

To make tools for the mind that advance humankind.

Backstory: Steve Jobs met Steve Wozniak at the Homebrew Computer Club, a gathering of enthusiasts in a garage in California's Menlo Park. Wozniak had seen his first MITS Altair there and was inspired by the build-it-yourself approach of the Altair kit to make something simpler for the rest of us. So he produced the first computer with a typewriter-like keyboard and the ability to connect to a regular TV. Later christened the Apple I, it was the archetype of every modern computer[35].

---

35. http://www.macworld.co.uk/feature/apple/history-of-apple-steve-jobs-what-happened-mac-computer-3606104/#foundation

RED GOLDFISH: DILLAN'S VOICE

Dillan Barnache was the star of a short film called Dillan's Voice. It was created by Apple to celebrate Autism Acceptance Day. The film tells Dillan's story as a nonverbal kid with autism through his own words. His words are typed out on an iPad and then spoken aloud using an augmented and alternative communication (AAC) app. In 2014, when Dillan used his tablet and an AAC app to deliver a moving middle school graduation speech, his use of the technology went viral. Apple is all about the use of its products as life-shifting technology, just as it is for Dillan. In an interview with Mashable, Sarah Herrlinger, senior manager for global accessibility policy and initiatives at Apple, said, "For Apple, accessibility is about empowering everyone to use our technology to be creative, productive and independent.[36]"

SUBCATEGORY: ARTISTIC DESIGNERS

These companies design beautiful products. While they are often not superior in their functionality, product features, or usability, these companies accentuate user experience through artistic interpretation. The customer is treated to an indulgent aesthetic interaction with the product because of its elegance and beauty.

2. METHOD HOME PURPOSE STATEMENT

To design a cleaner clean.

Backstory: Adam Lowry and Eric Ryan, childhood friends growing up in Grosse Pointe, Michigan, brainstormed ways to re-think common, established consumer goods. They decided soap needed re-invention. Lowry, a chemical engineer with an environmental degree, wanted to create safe, non-toxic soaps that were highly

---

36. http://mashable.com/2016/04/02/apple-autism-dillan/#k4dzdbgxPSq8

effective and would appeal to customers beyond the tiny market of "tree-hugging granola greenies" who purchased "safe" soaps in not so attractive packaging out of grim concern for the environment. Ryan, who had done edgy advertising for Gap, Saturn, and other big brands, wanted to package the soaps in ergonomically designed, environmentally responsible bottles that were stylish, playful, and made of eco-friendly materials that customers would feel great about using. Using $100,000 of their own savings, the duo set out to create a better cleaning product and pleasing packaging for it. They began whipping up batches of liquid soaps in their apartment bathtub and shopping them around to distributors. When the 2001 recession hit, retailers played it safe with familiar cleaning products. In 2002, Method got a test market project in 90 Target stores. There was an overwhelming response. Within seven months, Method's cleaning sprays and dish soaps were selling in Target stores nationwide. "Method casts itself as much as a social movement as it is a for-profit company," says Chris Malone, author of *The Human Brand*[37].

RED GOLDFISH: OCEAN PLASTIC

It's estimated that several million tons of plastic make their way into our oceans every year, polluting the environment and hurting our marine populations. And the problem isn't going away anytime soon, as more plastic washes up on beaches everyday. Method raises awareness about the issue and uses their business to demonstrate smart ways of using and reusing the plastics that are already on the planet. They enlist the help of local beach clean-up groups and volunteers to collect plastic from the beaches of Hawaii. Method works with Envision Plastics, a recycling partner, to turn this collected plastic into bottles. By recycling and reusing existing plastic,

37. http://fidelum.com/newsletter/method-products-the-power-of-passion-and-purpose/

Method's packaging materials make not only a design statement but also improve the health of our oceans[38].

3. IDEO PURPOSE STATEMENT

To create positive impact by design.

Backstory: After earning a master's degree from Stanford, David Kelley formed his own design firm in 1978 with fellow student Dean Hovey. The group's first studio was above a dress shop in Palo Alto. They made their own furnishings and covered the floors with green patio carpet. Kelley had met Apple Computer Inc. founder Steve Jobs at Stanford, and by 1983, the group had designed the first commercially available computer mouse for Apple's Lisa computer. Reports have it that a butter dish and the ball from a bottle of roll-on deodorant were among the building blocks for the first prototypes. In mid-1991, David Kelley Design merged with ID Two and Matrix Product Design to form IDEO Product Development, Inc. ID Two's Bill Moggridge was the one who picked the name out of the dictionary, according to the book *The Art of Innovation*. "IDEO" is the combining form of the word "idea," as in "ideology" or "ideogram." Today the company has over 200 employees in nine offices around the world[39].

RED GOLDFISH: OPENIDEO - A PLATFORM TO HARNESS COLLABORATION FOR SOCIAL GOOD

OpenIDEO is an open innovation platform where people from all corners of the world collaboratively tackle some of the toughest global issues through launching challenges, programs, and other tailored experiences. A challenge is a three-to-five month collaborative process that focuses attention on the topic and cre-

---

38. http://methodhome.com/beyond-the-bottle/ocean-plastic/

39. http://www.fundinguniverse.com/company-histories/ideo-inc-history/

ates a space for community members to contribute and build off each other. This approach is modeled on IDEO's design thinking methodology[40].

OpenIDEO is a Red Goldfish use of technology that harnesses collaborative help from all over the world to work to create positive impact through design, brand, build, and more just as put forth in their purpose.

SUBCATEGORY: PRODUCT FEATURE DESIGNERS

These companies take existing products and add new features to them that innovate the product line. The product features typically have a purpose-driven mission behind them such as products will be made green and sustainable. Products will include new features that empower constituencies. For example, Feelgoodz flip-flops are made from all natural rubber harvested in Thailand by empowered local people. These new product features often have an entire storyline behind them that gives the feature more appeal.

4. PAPER CULTURE PURPOSE STATEMENT

To design and deliver modern eco stationery as unique as the life events they help celebrate

Backstory: Christopher Wu had a honey-do list. Like most expectant fathers, Wu's wife assigned him a list of jobs to do when she was pregnant. He needed to paint the nursery, put the crib together, and order birth announcements. Her criteria for the announcements: get it done! His criteria: they had to be modern, made from 100% recycled premium paper, and the company had to address, hand stamp, and mail the announcements for him. The first two jobs on his wife's list were easy. When Wu could not find the right

---

40. https://www.ideo.com/post/a-platform-to-harness-collaboration-for-social-good

birth announcements, he decided to start his own company. Seven years after its inception, Paper Culture's Award winning designs have been featured around the world for their innovative style and eco-friendly mission. By printing on 100% post-consumer recycled paper, fabric and bamboo, operating CarbonFree, and planting a tree for every order (almost 400,000 so far), Paper Culture gives back to the environment with every design, allowing customers to create beautiful eco-friendly gifts, decorations, and holiday cards. Wu even makes it easy for busy moms and dads like himself to finish their to-do lists by offering Free Designer Assistance and Mail & Message, a service where Paper Culture will address, hand stamp, and mail cards for their customers.

RED GOLDFISH: FREE FULL SERVICE MAILING OPTION

With the free full service mailing option, Paper Culture addresses, stamps, and mails the customer's cards for only the cost of the stamps.

5. 3M PURPOSE STATEMENT

To solve unsolved problems innovatively

Backstory: Five businessmen founded Minnesota Mining and Manufacturing (3M) in Two Harbors, Minnesota in 1902. Originally a mining venture, it moved to the manufacture of sandpaper. When they had difficulties with product quality, they investigated, found a determinant problem, and came up with a solution to resolve it to improve their product quality. It seems that the garnets imported from Italy to make the grit for their sandpaper had been packed near olive oil, which had contaminated the stones. Unable to sustain the financial loss of discarding the product, the company decided to heat the stones to drive out the oil. This was their first company foray into research and development.

In 1923, 3M employee Richard Drew assumed the task of creating an adhesive that would not leave a residue or react adversely with paint to resolve a problem in an autobody shop where he had been testing the company's Wetordry sandpaper. Although he was encouraged to get back to basic business, Drew persisted with his research. The final result of that project was Scotch masking tape, but it was followed by more research and another new product: cellophane tape.

RED GOLDFISH: 15% TIME

After the development of masking tape, William McKnight, 3M CEO from 1949 to 1966, learned a crucial lesson about letting his engineers follow their instincts. The result of that lesson was a policy known as the 15% rule. "Encourage experimental doodling," he told his managers. "If you put fences around people, you get sheep. Give people the room they need." The 15% rule lets 3M engineers spend up to 15% of their work time pursuing whatever project they like[41]. The opportunity to devote time to pursuing fresh ideas is a Red Goldfish for employees but also benefits the world with innovative ways to solve problems, create new products, and get things done.

SUBCATEGORY: CUSTOMER EXPERIENCE DESIGNERS

These are companies that have revolutionized the customer experience, creating an entirely new interface with the business.

6. ZAPPOS PURPOSE STATEMENT

To deliver happiness.

---

41. http://money.cnn.com/magazines/fsb/fsb_archive/2003/04/01/341016/

Backstory: The year was 1998, and Zappos.com founder Nick Swinmurn was walking around a mall in San Francisco looking for a certain pair of brown Airwalk shoes. One store had the right style, but not the color. Another store had the color, but not the right size. Nick spent the next hour in the mall, walking from store to store, finally going home empty-handed and frustrated.

Nick didn't have any more luck at home, because although there were a lot of mom-and-pop stores selling shoes online, there were no major online retailers that specialized in shoes. Seeing both a need and an opportunity, Nick quit his day job and started an online shoe retailer, Shoesite.com. Nick did not want to prevent the business from being able to expand into other product categories, so he decided Shoesite.com needed a new name. "Nick…asked me what I thought of 'Zapos' as the name for the company, derived from zapatos, which was the Spanish word for "shoes," recalls Zappos CEO Tony Hsieh. "I told him that he should add another "p" to it so that people wouldn't mispronounce it and accidentally say ZAY-pos." It was 1999, and Zappos.com was born[42].

RED GOLDFISH: ZAPPOS FOR GOOD

Zappos partnered with Soles4Souls to create Zappos for Good. The program helps communities everywhere by sponsoring the cost of shipping donated shoes and clothing to Soles4Souls. The gently used items go to people in need rather than ending up in a landfill. Zappos thanks participating customers with 10% off their next Zappos.com purchase[43]. Zappos for Good is a two-fold Red Goldfish. By sponsoring the cost to ship donated shoes through Soles4Souls, not only does Zappos do good in the world, which is consistent with company culture and pleasing to the customer,

---

42. https://www.zapposinsights.com/about/zappos/the-zappos-story
43. https://secure-www.zappos.com/zapposforgood/give

but contributing customers also receive a Zappos' discount on their next purchase–delivering happiness in many directions.

7. DISNEY PURPOSE STATEMENT

To create the happiest place on Earth.

Backstory: Van Arsdale France saw his job as promoting an intangible dream. He was the founder of the "University of Disneyland" in 1955 to create a training program for everyone who would be part of the Disney experience. He had a clear vision of what the purpose of Disneyland should be: to create happiness for others. As he saw it, no matter what an employee's job was from parking cars to cleaning to everything else, it needed to be about more than the paycheck; it needed to be about creating happiness. He pitched that idea to the top executives at Disney, including Walt and Roy Disney. France's particular genius was in creating this single unifying principle to connect every Cast Member with the emotional aspirations of Disney guests. The purpose shines through in the extraordinary teamwork of the Disney Cast and their complete focus on the Disney guest. France called this common purpose their *raison d'etre*, their reason for being.

RED GOLDFISH: 3 O'CLOCK PARADE

Disney historian Les Perkins shared a story about Walt Disney at Disneyland during the early years of the park. In 1957, Walt decided to hold a Christmas parade at the new park at a cost of $350,000. Walt's accountants approached him and besieged him to not spend money on an extravagant Christmas parade because the people would already be there. Nobody would complain, they reasoned, if they dispensed with the parade because nobody would be expecting it. Walt's reply to his accountants is classic: "That's just the point," he said. "We should do the parade precisely because no one's expecting it. Our goal at Disneyland is to always give the people more than they expect. As long as we keep surprising them, they'll keep coming back. But if they ever stop coming, it'll cost us ten times that much to get them to come back."

They held that Christmas parade and soon it became a daily fixture at Disney parks. So much so that the #1 question asked at Disney is "What time is the 3 o'clock parade?[44]"

Disney carries out its purpose to create the happiest place on earth in many ways, but the account of the genesis of the 3 o'clock parade is a classic example of giving customers a Red Goldfish.

SUBCATEGORY: HIGH-TECH DESIGNERS

These are companies that have exceptional prowess in high-end industrial engineering and research. They are big-brained engineers who use complicated science and technology to solve complicated problems. They design new features and bring entirely new functionality to existing product lines and design breakthrough products using raw brainpower and hard work.

8. TESLA PURPOSE STATEMENT

To accelerate the advent of sustainable transport.

Backstory: In 2000, Martin Eberhard and Marc Tarpenning, co founders of NuvoMedia, took an unsolicited offer to buy their company for a purchase price of $187 million dollars. By late 2000, both were ready to start another company. Eberhard got divorced about that time and decided to buy a sports car. The sports car choices were reporting 18 miles to the gallon and that was unsatisfactory. The better option, a high-performance electric vehicle, didn't quite

---

44. https://www.amazon.com/How-Be-Like-Walt-Capturing/dp/0757302319

exist. Tarpenning and Eberhard knew that they wanted to found an electric-car company, starting with a two-seater sports car and then moving into more accessible markets. On Jan. 25, 2003, Eberhard went on a date to Disneyland with Carolyn, his now wife. They went to the Blue Bayou, a restaurant inside the Pirates of the Caribbean ride. It was about as romantic you could get at Disneyland. He had been pitching her on car-company names for months, but the right branding proved elusive. This was to be a high-performance car that happened to be electric, so any overly "eco" or "engineery" name sounded tone-deaf — volts, surges, and leaves would be set aside. It would have to be easy to say and remember, and sound like a car company, not another high-tech startup.

Eberhard wanted to give credit to the man who patented the type of motor he planned on using, the AC induction motor, invented by the Serbian-American genius Nikola Tesla. He said to her, "What about Tesla Motors?" Her reply: "Perfect! Now get to work making your car."

On March 31, 2004, Eberhard sent Elon Musk an email. "We would love to talk to you about Tesla Motors," he wrote, "particularly if you might be interested in investing in the company. I believe that you have driven AC Propulsion's tzero car. If so, you already know that a high-performance electric car can be made. We would like to convince you that we can do so profitably, creating a company with very high potential for growth, and at the same time breaking the compromise between driving performance and efficiency."

Musk replied that evening. "Sure," he said. "Friday this week or Friday next week would work." Eberhard and Ian Wright, the third member of their team, flew to Los Angeles, where SpaceX was based, and pitched Musk in his SpaceX office. The pitch was supposed to be 30 minutes, Eberhard recalled. It lasted two hours. Eberhard realized that Musk was the first guy he had met who shared his vision for electric cars: make a vastly superior car, not just a car that sucks less[45].

RED GOLDFISH: OPEN PATENTS

In a bold move in 2004, Tesla Motors made all the patents for the company's electric car technology free and available for anyone to use. Elon Musk said the decision to share the company's patents was made "in the spirit of the open source movement, for the advancement of electric vehicle technology. Tesla Motors was created to accelerate the advent of sustainable transport. If we clear a path to the creation of compelling electric vehicles, but then lay intellectual property landmines behind us to inhibit others, we are acting in a manner contrary to that goal." By making Tesla's patents open source, Musk hopes to bolster the electric car industry, which is still heavily outmuscled by traditional car companies, and make strides in stemming harmful emissions that are contributing to global warming. "Our true competition is not the small trickle of non-Tesla electric cars being produced, but rather the enormous flood of gasoline cars pouring out of the world's factories every day.[46]" Tesla's open patents move is a huge Red Goldfish for the design and production of a quality electric car and a serious statement toward the fulfillment of their purpose "to accelerate the advent of sustainable transport."

SUBCATEGORY: PROTECTING DESIGNERS

These companies seek to produce products designed to protect something or to create those products in a way that is more sustainable for the planet. Tom Organic wants to produce personal hygiene products free of toxins. Waste management wants to re-

---

45. http://www.businessinsider.com/tesla-the-origin-story-2014-10

46. http://www.livescience.com/46301-tesla-patents-open-source.html

duce the impact that trash has on the planet. D.light created a solar powered light that protects third-world families from the dangers of burning kerosene.

9. TOM ORGANIC PURPOSE STATEMENT

To pioneer a range of pure and essential personal care products that respect the environment and empower women to live healthier, more fulfilled lives.

Backstory: Aimee Marks was working on a high school design project when she became aware of the pesticides and synthetics used in the materials and production of conventional tampons and pads. She quickly made it her mission to create feminine hygiene products that had a positive impact. Marks enrolled in a business entrepreneurship program to pursue her idea. In 2009, TOM Organic was born, giving women access to pure, reliable organic tampons and pads. The TOM product range has evolved as Aimee and her team have become increasingly in touch with women's personal care needs[47].

RED GOLDFISH: TOM ORGANIC JOURNAL

The TOM Organic Journal is an online blog geared toward customers. Posts follow six categories: Cook, Green, Health, Inspire, Lifestyle, and TOM Loves.

The next archetype is The Guide.

---

47. http://tomorganic.com/au/our-story/our-founder/

CHAPTER 10

THE GUIDE

*"It is every man's obligation to put back into the world
at least the equivalent of what he takes out of it."*

— Albert Einstein

The fourth archetype is The Guide. The purpose of The Guide is rooted in Maslow's concept of love. The goal is to help facilitate individual progress.

Type: Love

Category: Product to Purpose

Archetype: The Guide - Facilitating individual progress

Fiction: Mr. Miyagi, Glinda

Non-Fiction: Salman Kahn, Neil Degrasse Tyson, Seth Godin

The symbol of The Guide is Mr. Miyagi from the movie *The Karate Kid*. Brands with The Guide archetype are teachers. They want to help others navigate the world. They are wired to educate. In the words of Mr. Miyagi after Daniel asked if he could teach him the crane technique, "First learn stand, then learn fly. Nature rule, Daniel-san, not mine."

The Guide archetype can be broken down to the following four subcategories:

•   Information empowerers: Google

•   Teachers: Khan Academy, Fidelity Charitable

•   Champions: Boston Beer, d.light

•   Nurturers: King Arthur Flour

Let's look at six brands that have embraced The Guide archetype. To see more examples of this archetype, visit the Red Goldfish online resource library where you'll find hundreds of great examples, training videos, and more case studies. Go to 602communications. com/redgoldfish

SUBCATEGORY: INFORMATION EMPOWERERS

The Information empowerers are companies focused on the power of information. They believe that by getting the right information into the hands of everyday people, amazing things are possible. They are believers in smart, better thinking driven by the best information on the planet. They believe in the enlightening and rejuvenating potential of data and feel that any person in the world is made better when the facts are available to them at the right time in the right place.

1. GOOGLE PURPOSE STATEMENT

To organize the world's information and make it universally accessible.

Backstory: In 1995 at age 22, Larry Page met Sergey Brin at Stanford. Within a year, the two begin to collaborate on a search engine - named BackRub - that they hosted on the university's servers. On-September 17, 1997, they registered a new domain name for their search engine: Google, a play on the math term googol (1 followed by 100 zeros). Their inspiration for the name was their mission to organize the ever-growing amount of information on the web[48].

---

48. https://www.google.com/about/company/history/

RED GOLDFISH: TGIF

Google is committed to keeping employees up to speed on the state of business and has been since the beginning. One of Google's first and most famous perks is their Friday afternoon business-update-beer-bash named "TGIF." Google's business leaders, and even the founders, gather to deliver in-person business updates to employees. These candid conversations from the mouths of company leaders keep employees connected to the company's goals, challenges, and opportunities, which helps keep them tied to purpose as well. It's noteworthy that TGIF now takes place on Thursdays so employees in Google's Asian offices can dial-in for the business update[49]. The concept behind TGIF is to help employees stay in the loop so they can understand where the company is going and can better help it get there, to keep organizing information for everyone to access.

SUBCATEGORY: TEACHERS

The Teachers are organizations that actively seek to educate and teach people specific skills that will empower them to move forward in their lives. There is a spirit of protection that underlies this as well. These teachers are often bringing people out of ignorance and the dangers of exploitation. They are there to provide learning and education that will empower people to make better choices and to prosper.

2. KHAN ACADEMY PURPOSE STATEMENT

To provide free, world-class education for anyone, anywhere.

Backstory: In 2004, Salman Khan offered to help his 12-year-old cousin Nadia with her math to keep her from getting tracked into

---

49. http://www.greatplacetowork.net/publications-and-events/blogs-and-news/1630

a slower math class. His plan was to tutor her by telephone. Word spread within the family about his "free tutoring," and Khan found himself doing math tutoring for 15 cousins by phone. He created a website where his cousins could go to practice problems and where he could suggest things for them to work on. During his telephone tutoring session, he would use Yahoo Doodle, a program that was part of Yahoo Messenger, so his cousins could see the calculations on their computers while they talked. Two years later, a friend inquired about how Khan was scaling his lessons. When Khan said he wasn't, the friend suggested that he make videos of the tutorials and post them on YouTube. Khan apparently initially replied, "That's a horrible idea. YouTube is for cats playing piano." However, he did make some videos and post them. They were well received by his cousins because they could watch them whenever they wanted and not have to worry about being judged in the group.

Since the videos were free and open for viewing on YouTube, other people found their way to the videos as well. By 2008, tens of thousands of students were watching his videos every month. In 2009, Khan left his job at a hedge fund and began building the Khan Academy[50].

RED GOLDFISH: KHAN LAB SCHOOL

Khan Lab School is an actual physical school that teaches students based on the Khan Academy "One World Schoolhouse" philosophy. The Lab School works to develop personalized, student-based teaching practices and empowers students to take ownership of their learning[51]. Education is clearly a place where information empowers for the archetype. This Red Goldfish from Khan Academy provides a real time environment for developing innovative learning, leading "to a world-class education for everyone, everywhere."

50. https://www.nytimes.com/2014/01/28/science/salman-khan-turned-family-tutoring-into-khan-academy.html?_r=0
51. http://khanlabschool.org/about

3. FIDELITY CHARITABLE PURPOSE STATEMENT

To help clients with their philanthropic goals with a smarter way to give to charity.

Backstory: Fidelity Charitable was founded in 1991 based on an idea from the chairman of Fidelity Investments. The idea was to create a product called a Giving Account. With a Giving Account, donations to Fidelity Charitable are tax-deductible. The money in the account is a donor-advised fund. Account owners advise Fidelity Charitable on how to grant the money out to the requested charities. The donations are invested based on client preferences, so funds have the potential to grow, tax-free, while the client is deciding which charities to support. Today, Fidelity Charitable works with over 100,000 donors to support more than 200,000 charities and make more of a difference every day.

RED GOLDFISH: CHARITABLE PLANNING PRACTICE MANAGEMENT

Charitable Planning Practice Management helps advisors assist clients with their philanthropic goals. This educational and counseling program is designed to help financial advisors sharpen their skills in holistic financial planning by helping their clients address and manage philanthropy decisions. With an estimated 27 percent of $30 trillion to be transferred to the heirs of the boomer generation, charitable planning will be a sought-after skill. Advisors who add this dimension to their financial planning practice can differentiate themselves from other advisors as they build credibility and earn the trust of the next generation. This Red Goldfish benefits charitable organizations with planned giving and benefits advisors by teaching them how to help their clients realize their philanthropic goals with the added dimension for the client of actually growing the charitable account tax-free[52]!

SUBCATEGORY: CHAMPIONS

The Champions are typically founders who have taken on a cause or constituency with the idea of nurturing to bring it to its full potential. This could be a profession, a vocation, a group, or any other institution. These businesses openly advocate for their constituencies, actively fostering and facilitating their progress. D.light advocates for the poor people of the world by providing renewable solar energy lights that empower them to learn, spend time together, and avoid the dangers of kerosene. Sam Adams believes in beer culture and fostering knowledge and appreciation of beer.

4. D.LIGHT PURPOSE STATEMENT

Power the world with universal access to energy.

Backstory: Here is an excerpt from d.light's company website: The Story of Sam

> In 2004, Sam Goldman was a Peace Corps volunteer in Benin, West Africa, when tragedy struck his neighbors. Sam was living in a remote, un-electrified village called Guinagourou. He had come to rely on a small LED headlamp for light each evening; the other households in the village only had access to kerosene lanterns.
>
> One evening, a young boy living in the hut next door accidentally spilled a burning kerosene lamp. He sustained third-degree burns over his entire body. The

---

52. http://www.fa-mag.com/news/fidelity-charitable-adds-practice-management-education-28164.html

nearest hospital was forty-five kilometers away. With no ambulance support outside the cities, Sam watched as the neighbors gathered to offer their condolences and local herbs to ease the boy's pain.

Sam was horrified by what kerosene had done to this boy and his family, and wondered why simple technology like his LED headlamp was not more readily available. He had grown up in India, Pakistan, Peru, Mauretania, and Africa with his aid-worker parents, and understood that many people still lacked access to reliable electricity. Neither the public nor the private sectors were adequately meeting this huge need.

"This ten-dollar light had transformed my life," Sam recalls. "Instead of buying kerosene, I could save a good percentage of my small Peace Corps stipend. I could see to cook and read comfortably without inhaling kerosene fumes or worrying about the mosquito net catching fire. I was safer because I was able to avoid being bitten by snakes or scorpions."

Sam contacted multiple corporations that sold portable lights in hopes of becoming a distributor, but no one responded. He decided to bring the technology to Africa himself[53].

Sam enrolled in the Design for Extreme Affordability program at the Stanford Design School. He and fellow classmate Ned Tozun created the first prototype for lighting for families without electricity: a simple, battery-powered LED light. After graduating in 2007, they turned that class project into d.light design, now called d.light, a for-profit social enterprise with the purpose of providing bright,

---

53. http://www.dlight.com/blog/founding-story/

affordable solar light to the 1.6 billion people worldwide who lack access to electricity.

RED GOLDFISH: ENERGY ACCESS ACCELERATOR

The Energy Access Accelerator is an initiative focused on integrating the company's growing range of solar power products and services with a diversity of payment and distribution systems. Pay-as-you-go is no longer novel in the solar industry, but d.light's innovation is having a variety of payment options, so a market can find an option that is suitable from top-up cards, microloans, mobile money, cash, employer-sponsored plans, or savings and credit groups[54].

The combination of the right products to serve the market and the methods through d.light's Red Goldfish Energy Access Accelerator to make the products affordable works powerfully toward to company's purpose "to power the world with universal access to energy."

5. BOSTON BEER PURPOSE STATEMENT

To promote brewing as an artful craft.

Backstory: The Boston Beer Company was founded in 1984 by Jim Koch, a sixth-generation brewmaster and former Bain consultant. Koch brewed a beer recipe from his great-great grandfather. He named the brew Samuel Adams Boston Lager after the patriot and revolutionary. Two months after Samuel Adams Boston Lager was first offered, it was picked the best beer in America at the Great American Beer Festival in Denver. Hoping to change what drinkers thought of beer, which at the time was mass-produced and not particularly flavorful, the first cases of Samuel Adams Boston La-

---

54. http://www.forbes.com/sites/eshachhabra/2014/08/12/bite-size-payments-go-global-solars-next-challenge/#5e50c6df73fe

ger were sold in Boston on Patriot's Day in 1985. When Koch first started the company, his original business plan called for brewing 5,000 barrels of beer by the end of year five. However, by 1988, The Boston Beer Company was brewing 36,000 barrels and was selling its beer on both coasts. In 2015, the company sold more than 4.3 million barrels of core products, making The Boston Beer Company one of the largest craft breweries in the United States[55].

RED GOLDFISH: BREWING THE AMERICAN DREAM

In June 2008, Jim Koch created Samuel Adams Brewing the American Dream, a philanthropic program that champions small businesses nationwide in the food and beverage, hospitality, and craft brewing industries. They teamed with non-profit microlender Accion to combine expert business coaching and advice as well as access to small business capital. Through Samuel Adams Speed Coaching, small business owners in food, beverage, and brewing can get expert, personalized business advice that they otherwise wouldn't be able to access[56].

Creating a program to promote the growth and well-being of small business owners in the hospitality industry is a worthy Red Goldfish that will benefit business owners and thereby their customers and promote good will for Samuel Adams Brewing.

SUBCATEGORY: NURTURERS

This subcategory is a combination of the advocates and the teachers. The nurturers focus on providing a holistically optimal environment for growth to a given constituency. They will shepherd them through the years, constantly monitoring their progress and keeping them on track with advice, education, and mentoring.

---

55. http://www.bostonbeer.com/phoenix.zhtml?c=69432&p=irol-faq-company
56. http://btad.samueladams.com/about

They are in it for the long haul. There is a maternal/paternal bent about their demeanor. They want to create an environment that will allow people to grow and prosper. The leaders of these companies are typically people who have experienced a profound event in their life that could be one of joy or one of sorrow. This has left a mark on them and shows them how important it is to help others navigate their way through the challenges that life inevitably will bring.

6. KING ARTHUR FLOUR PURPOSE STATEMENT

To use baking to make a change in the world.

Backstory: In 1790, Henry Wood began importing European flour to Long Wharf in Boston, Massachusetts. His goal was to provide high-quality flour for bakers in the fledgling United States. More than 100 years later, the company Wood founded gave its product a new brand name: King Arthur Flour. In 1984, owners Frank and Brinna Sands moved the company from Massachusetts, where it had been based for 194 years, to Norwich, Vermont, where the company is headquartered today. In 1996, the company started an Employee Stock Ownership Plan. By 2004, the company was 100% employee owned. In 2007, King Arthur Flour became a founding B Corporation, changing its bylaws to reflect its commitment to all stakeholders–including shareholders, business partners, the community, and the environment[57].

RED GOLDFISH: BAKE FOR GOOD

The King Arthur Flour Bake for Good program teaches kids from fourth to seventh grade to make bread from scratch. The King Arthur Flour formula is "math + science + reading + baking know-how = something delicious!" Sometimes King Arthur Flour in-

---

57. http://www.kingarthurflour.com/about/history.html

structors visit schools and sometimes the program is self-directed. The company provides each child with a bag of ingredients. The kids practice their new skills and use the ingredients to bake bread or rolls. At the end of the program, participating kids share with the community, giving part of their baked goods to those in need. In the 25 years the program has been in place, over 300,000 kids have participated. "Part of our mission as a company is to give back to the community, so this program is a win-win for everybody. It empowers kids to make a difference, which can be difficult to do when you're only nine. It teaches them a skill that they can really use forever," says Paula Gray, manager of the Bake for Good Program[58]. The King Arthur Flour Bake for Good Red Goldfish reaches children in a way that instills confidence in learning a new skill, giving them experience with sharing what they have with others, and, through this, the program exemplifies the company's purpose "to use baking to make a change in the world."

The next archetype is The Advocate.

---

[58]. http://www.coastalpoint.com/content/%E2%80%98bake-good%E2%80%99-helps-local-food-kitchen_09_01_2016

CHAPTER 11

THE ADVOCATE

"My goal, as I saw it, was to get everyone we hired to share in an intangible dream, and not just working for a paycheck."

— Van Arsdale France,
Founder of the University of Disneyland

The fifth archetype is The Advocate. The purpose of The Advocate is rooted in Maslow's concept of love. The goal is to help advocate for a tribe.

Type: Love

Category: Product to Purpose

Archetype: The Advocate - Those who advocate for a tribe

Fiction: Atticus Finch, Katniss Everdeen

Non-Fiction: Susan Komen, Sheryl Sandberg, Michelle Obama, MLK, Oskar Schindler

The symbol of The Advocate is Atticus Finch from *To Kill A Mockingbird*. Brands with The Advocate archetype are passionate supporters. They want to stand up for certain groups of people in this world. They are wired to fight. In the words of the lawyer Atticus Finch, "You'll decide you don't like the taste of injustice, not for you and not for anyone, and you'll understand that even though all the battles can't be won, that doesn't mean you won't fight."

This archetype can be broken into the following subcategories:

- Advocating for an empowered constituency: AARP, Pedigree

- Helping the misfortunate: Krochet Kids, Panera Bread

- Honoring service: Johnson & Johnson, Mission BBQ

- Empowering through education: Fuller Cut

- Empowering a cause: Intrepid Travel

- Defending the powerless: Meathead Movers

COOPERATIVES: REI, BROOKLYN CO-OP

Let's look at 11 brands that have embraced The Advocate archetype. To see more examples of this archetype, visit the Red Goldfish online resource library where you'll find hundreds of great examples, training videos, and more case studies. Go to 602communications. com/redgoldfish

SUBCATEGORY: ADVOCATES FOR AN EMPOWERED CONSTITUENCY

Advocates for an empowered constituency cheerlead for a group. These businesses have aligned themselves with passionate tribes who love each other and are proud to be a member of their group.

1. AARP PURPOSE STATEMENT

To fight for and equip each individual to live their best life.

Backstory: In 1947, private health insurance was unavailable for nearly all older Americans. (Medicare would not be enacted by the US government until 1965.) A retired high principal named Ethel Percy Andrus took exception to this and created an organization she called the National Retired Teachers Association (NRTA). Her goal was not only to provide for health insurance needs for retired teachers but also to foster productive retirement time. Though it was not easy, Dr. Andrus found an insurance company willing to insure older Americans, then she moved on to add a discount pharmacy and a number of other benefits. All this did not go unnoticed by other retired Americans over the next ten years. As demand for the service increased, Dr. Andrus opened the organization to all retired Americans and NRTA became the American Association of Retired Persons or AARP[59].

RED GOLDFISH: LIFE REIMAGINED

Life Reimagined is a community from AARP that helps retired people find a focus for something they really want to do. A variety of experts in the areas of well-being and relationships provide leadership and guidance to members to shape and define their new phase of life[60].

This AARP Red Goldfish program offers help to retired people to find a new lease on life and, by those actions, enriches the communities benefiting from the purpose of "living best lives."

2. PEDIGREE PURPOSE STATEMENT

To do everything for the love of dogs.

Backstory: In 1936, Clement L. Hirsch founded the Dog Town Packing Company inVernon, California. During World War II, the Company became Victory Packing Company, supplying food for U.S. war dogs. Its introduction of a canned all-meat pet food in the 1940's helped to pioneer the high quality pet food business of today. In 1957, the Company changed its name to Kal Kan Foods, Inc. It continued to grow and prosper during the early sixties, introducing new products while increasing distribution on existing Kal Kan brands. In 1968, Mars, Incorporated acquired Kal Kan. In the early 2000's, the brand managers at Mars' Masterfoods decided

---

59. http://www.aarp.org/about-aarp/company/info-2016/history.html
60. https://lifereimagined.aarp.org/who-we-are

they needed a new campaign. They turned to agency TBWA\Chi-at\Day for ideas. Agency lead Lee Clow proposed a redesign that challenged the entire way the company operated. Clow shared his thinking in an interview with one:design. Here is an excerpt from the article:

> With Pedigree, we had to help them to discover their culture and behavior. Over the years, we've kind of formalized how we believe iconic brands are created—and the first piece involves understanding what a brand truly believes, as opposed to what it makes or sells. In the case of Pedigree, we felt the belief system should be, 'Everything we do is for the love of dogs.' It was a credo that rang true in terms of the values and the history of the brand. (Pedigree was among the first to offer packaged pet food as a healthier alternative to feeding dogs table scraps, and the brand was also known as a favorite among dog breeders.) But it hadn't been expressed in Pedigree's external communications to the world. And even internally, Pedigree needed to do a better job of instilling the idea among its people that they worked for a company that was focused on the well being of dogs, as opposed to one that just made dog food. Clow had advised Pedigree that if it intended to be a company for dog-lovers, it should "walk the walk" by implementing dog-friendly policies in its own workplace. The company began to encourage associates to bring their dogs to work—and as part of that effort, the agency helped redesign ID badges and business cards so that they featured images of employees' dogs. Pedigree also began to extend healthcare benefits to associates' dogs—opening the door for the company to become an advocate for other companies in other industries to consider doing likewise. Life at

Pedigree changed overnight as all the offices "went to the dogs." Dogs were now part of the workday environment and portraits of dogs adorned the walls. The company also stepped up its involvement in dog-related issues and causes, most notably its support of shelter dogs. Perhaps the biggest payoff is the one Clow observed in the people who work for the company. "They used to come to work every day thinking they worked for a dog food company," he said, "and now they come in thinking they work for a company that loves dogs[61]."

RED GOLDFISH: PEDIGREE FEEDING PROJECT

Pedigree founded The Pedigree Feeding Project to provide shelter dogs with a consistent, nutritious diet, helping them stay happy and healthy as they wait to find a forever home. Pedigree provides food to shelters in the program at absolutely no cost, allowing the shelters to use their limited resources to find loving homes for more of their dogs. The food that is provided is especially important to shelter dogs that often have not had good care. The nutritious supplied Pedigree food provides a diet that helps support the overall health of dogs with a focus in four key areas: skin & coat, oral care, digestion, and immunity. This project carries out in a powerful way Pedigree's purpose: To do everything for the love of dogs[62].

SUBCATEGORY: HELPING THE MISFORTUNATE

Companies in this category have selected groups that truly need help. The help is admirable, but it is not central to their business model. This is typical of a company that has been a traditional Mil-

---

61. https://www.scribd.com/presentation/70639736/Get-close-to-the-customer-Pedigree-Foods

62. http://www.pedigree.com/03Adoption/feeding-project/Default.aspx

ton Friedman focused business but is now trying to move into a purpose driven state. What is missing is any kind of central purpose driven from the top down. Most of these purposes are bottom-up where they are picking a purpose that somehow meshes well with their current business operation. Since these purposes did not start at the top, they will most likely continue to be charitable giving operations and not systemic purpose driven leadership. Still, these are good companies. They are early in their journey to instill purpose into their brands.

3. KROCHET KIDS PURPOSE STATEMENT

To put a human signature and face on a faceless industry.

Backstory: Kohl Crecelius, Travis Hartanov, and Stewart Ramsey, California surfers and skiers from a young age, also became avid beanie crocheters and, in college, world travelers doing good along the way. Eventually they founded Krochet Kids International, a non-profit with an apparel line. They taught 10 Ugandan women in a destitute government camp how to crochet, so they could be hired to make trendy cold-weather hats. Krochet Kids began producing lines of men's, women's, and kids' casual apparel, bags, and other accessories. This allowed Krochet Kids to expand and hire women in Lima, Peru, as well as Uganda to manufacture goods from materials sourced there. Their goal is to teach people living in poverty skills and resources so they can support themselves independently.

RED GOLDFISH: A NAME TAG

All of Krochet Kids' goods feature an inner tag that's signed by the woman who made the item. The company's website shares profiles of the women who make the bags and hats so customers can connect to their product's crafter. Customers can even leave thank you notes for the women[63]. Adding the name tag to the hat or bag and hosting profiles for the women who create the products "puts a human signature and face on a faceless industry" in a heart-warming way.

4. PANERA PURPOSE STATEMENT

To help people live consciously and eat deliciously.

Backstory: In 1993, Au Bon Pain Co., Inc. purchased Saint Louis Bread Company®, a chain of 20 bakery-cafes located in the St. Louis area. The company then managed a comprehensive re-staging of Saint Louis Bread Co. Between 1993 and 1997 average unit volumes increased by 75%. Ultimately the concept's name was changed to Panera Bread. By 1997, it was clear that Panera Bread had the potential to become one of the leading brands in the nation. In order for Panera Bread to reach its potential, it would require all the company's financial and management resources. In May 1999, all of Au Bon Pain Co., Inc.'s business units were sold with the exception of Panera Bread, and the company was renamed Panera Bread[64].

RED GOLDFISH: PANERA CARES

Panera Cares community cafes are a 501(c)3 organization to offer a meal to anyone who comes in, regardless of whether they can pay. They do operate on a pay-what-you-can model, providing suggested donation amounts for their menu items, but those who cannot pay are fed free. The funds collected cover operating costs but also cover the cost of meals for those who come to eat but who cannot pay or cannot pay the suggested amount. The cafes help raise

---

63. https://www.krochetkids.org/
64. https://www.panerabread.com/en-us/company/about-panera/our-history.html

awareness about the widespread problem of hunger in our own country[65].

Panera's Red Goldfish feeds those who need food, an enacted part of their purpose "to help people... eat deliciously."

SUBCATEGORY: HONORING SERVICE

These are incredibly positive brands that do not bemoan the bad things in the world but stand up and applaud for those doing their part to make the world a better place. Typically, these are lauded members of the community including policemen, soldiers, firefighters, doctors, volunteers, etc. These campaigns honor these people and hold them up as exemplary members of society. Typically, these companies then go on to advocate for them in some way. This could include helping the constituency with problems that are common to the group, financial contributions, or support services.

5. JOHNSON & JOHNSON PURPOSE STATEMENT

To improve care by taking care of the doctors, nurses, and patients we serve.

Backstory: It's a cold January day in 1886, and James Wood Johnson, one of the founders of Johnson & Johnson, is on a train heading from New York to Philadelphia. Early in 1885, Johnson and his brothers Robert and Edward had left their former company Seabury & Johnson with the intention of starting a new business. James was looking for a location. When the train stopped at a tiny station halfway through the journey, Johnson & Johnson found its hometown: the city of New Brunswick, New Jersey. In 1886, New Brunswick was a center of entrepreneurial and industrial activity

---

65. http://paneracares.org/our-mission/

thanks to three things: the railroad, the city's position on the Raritan River and Delaware-Raritan Canal, and its placement halfway between New York and Philadelphia. The city's approximately five square miles boasted a thriving, nationally-known wallpaper manufacturer, a fruit jar manufacturer, and a box manufacturer (both of which became packaging suppliers to Johnson & Johnson!), an iron works, the Edison Illuminating Company, a hosiery manufacturer, a carriage factory, and more. Johnson & Johnson would join the city's fledgling first hospital, founded 1884, in forming the nucleus of New Brunswick's significant health care presence today. When the Pennsylvania Railroad steam locomotive huffed to a stop at the little railroad depot bordered by George and Hamilton Streets in New Brunswick, Johnson looked out the window at the cold January landscape. About 150 feet back from the tracks, past the distinctive oval "Look Out for the Locomotive" street signs, Johnson noticed a four-story red brick building with a walk-in basement, a distinctive square chimney, arched windows and a "For Rent" sign. It was the former Janeway & Carpender wallpaper factory, outgrown by one of the city's thriving businesses that had moved to larger quarters. Johnson got off the train to take a closer look, and he ended up renting the top floor of the building for Johnson & Johnson. The company was named for himself and his brother Edward Mead Johnson[66].

RED GOLDFISH: EVERY NEWBORN ACTION PLAN

Through its Every Newborn Action Plan, Johnson & Johnson committed $30 million to improve newborn health and increase newborn survival through 2020. Programs will be supported in at least 20 countries where there is high newborn mortality. The countries will include early attention to India, Nigeria, China, and Ethiopia.

66. https://www.jnj.com/our-heritage/130-years-ago-james-wood-johnson-arrives-in-new-brunswick

Birth attendants will receive training and strategies will be introduced to reduce infant death from birth asphyxia, to work with
newborns at-risk for HIV, and to expand programs to deliver health
care information for safe-pregnancy and birth by mobile phones[67].
This very important Red Goldfish to help newborns survive by
improving birth attendant training and providing better natal care
and infant care to pregnant women and mothers carries out the
Johnson and Johnson purpose "to take care of doctors, nurses, and
patients" the company serves.

6. MISSION BBQ PURPOSE STATEMENT

To honor and serve those who serve.

Backstory: MISSION BBQ opened its doors for business on September 11, 2011, ten years after the infamous 9/11. The founders,
Steve Newton and Bill Kraus, honor the brave men and women
who have sworn to protect and serve our nation and our communities: our soldiers, firefighters, police officers, first responders. They
serve authentic BBQ in a patriotic dining room filled with tributes
to those who serve, given to them by the people who earned them.
From 40 locations in 2016 across 11 states, Mission BBQ plans to
have 80 restaurants by 2018.

RED GOLDFISH: AMERICAN HEROES CUPS

Mission BBQ offers American Heroes Cups to customers for a $2
donation that always goes to a charity supporting veterans and
first-responders. To date, MISSION BBQ and their loyal customers
have donated over $3 million to local charities in their communi-
ties since they opened in 2011. The Red Goldfish American Hero
Cups provides Mission BBQ customers an easy way to support vet-

---

67. http://www.everywomaneverychild.org/commitment/johnson-johnson/

eran and first responder causes while allowing the company to live strong in its purpose "to honor and serve those who serve."

SUBCATEGORY: EMPOWERING THROUGH EDUCATION

These organizations seek to educate their constituents in a mentoring role. They believe that the way forward can be bold and prosperous if the right information is provided and the members of the group are carefully schooled in the best way forward. These are paternal and maternal brands that seek to protect their constituents and empower them with knowledge to prosper.

7. FULLER CUT PURPOSE STATEMENT

To promote literacy and cultural awareness for kids.

Backstory: Alex Fuller, lifelong resident of Ypsilanti, Michigan, has owned a barbershop since 1994. Twenty odd years after his first shop, he opened The Fuller Cut, still going strong today. Over the years, he has purchased his own building, renovated and remodeled it, and hired great barbers. But what makes his shop special is his Red Goldfish[68].

RED GOLDFISH: TWO DOLLAR REBATE

Thanks to barber Ryan Griffin, a 20 year veteran at the Fuller Cut barbershop, kids who read books aloud to their barbers while they're getting their hair done get $2.00. Griffin said he had heard about reading programs other barbershops around the country and was inspired to bring a reading program to Fuller Cut. The shop collection started when he began to bring in old books from

---

68. http://www.thefullercut.com/about-us.html

his own children to the shop. There are 75-100 rotating titles the children can choose nowadays. Griffin reports that one of the best things about this program is that it shows kids that it is cool to read. "All our books have positive images of African-Americans — whether it's astronauts, athletes or writers," Griffin said. The community has embraced the idea. The shop has gotten new customers specifically because they've heard about the reading program, and older kids like to bring in their old books for the shop to use. But that's not even the best part. "When little kids that don't really know how to read or what's going on see an older kid in the chair with a book and then grab a book too, that's what's important," said Griffin to The Huffington Post. "Because when a kid thinks it's cool to read, that's a gift[69]."

SUBCATEGORY: EMPOWERING A CAUSE

Empowering a cause companies are dedicated to their own common mission. The brand needs to be clearly understandable and have a clear constituency that they serve. Companies here need to look at their organizational culture, assess what the people in their business believe, look at ways they can help, and then build their purpose from that central desire to help. This will make the mission/brand/purpose more authentic and will be more implementable by the team. Building a purpose driven business is challenging. If the purpose is at all fuzzy, it will probably fail.

8. INTREPID TRAVEL PURPOSE STATEMENT

To promote indigenous travel to support sustainable tourism.

Backstory: In 1988, two friends from Melbourne, Australia, did something they loved to do; they traveled. Darrell and Manch headed

---

69. http://www.huffingtonpost.com/entry/barbershop-michigan-discount-kids-read-books_us_57fe5bffe4b0162c043921ca

for Africa. They modified an ex-council truck, added friends, beer, aviator sunglasses, and supplies and hit the road. The story goes that somewhere along the way, they put on their world-changing sombreros and begin to think travel tour thoughts. Intrepid Travel was the result of all that. Today, the company sends over 100,000 travellers across the globe each year and employs more than 1,000 staff, traveling over 800 different itineraries across Europe, Asia, Africa, North & South America, the Middle East, Australia, and both the Arctic & Antarctica[70].

RED GOLDFISH: RESPONSIBLE TRAVEL

Responsible travel is an attitude promoted by Intrepid Travel. They guide tours, yes, but they do so keeping in mind the dignity of the local population and consideration for its culture, and they work to benefit the local economy and protect the local environment. The company's Red Goldfish enhances the travel experience for the Intrepid Travel client by incorporating their values in the travel to elevate traveler awareness and to sustain local cultures and economies.

The following list from the Intrepid Travel website reflects their responsible travel points:

• Using public transport where possible

• Staying in smaller-scale locally owned accommodations where possible

• Buying locally produced food and drink, and purchasing souvenirs from local artisans

• Spreading economic benefits by patronizing a range of suppliers

---

70. http://www.intrepidtravel.com/us/about/our-story

- Minimizing plastic waste where possible

- Careful management of limited energy and water resources

- Offering real life experiences which promote cross-cultural understanding

- Avoiding the exploitation of the vulnerable - including women, children, animals and endangered species[71]

SUBCATEGORY: DEFENDING THE POWERLESS

Defending the powerless companies actively seek to defend people from misfortune. They have a protective advocacy role as opposed to a nurturer advocacy role.

9. MEATHEAD MOVERS PURPOSE STATEMENT

To support college student athletes and assist victims of domestic violence with a fresh start

Backstory: Aaron and Evan Steed started Meathead Movers in 1997 as high school athletes needing to earn extra cash. Their founding principle was to support student athletes working their way through college, and they say that principle will remain even as they grow. Their credo is to work hard, have fun, and serve their community by providing premium moving services as well as assisting victims of domestic violence with a fresh start in life[72].

RED GOLDFISH: #MOVETOENDDV

Meathead Movers found itself receiving calls from frightened women needing help to move their belongings while their abuser

71. http://www.intrepidtravel.com/us/about/responsible-business

72. http://www.meatheadmovers.com/our-team/mission.aspx

was out of the house–which the company did for free. After an incident in 2000 that became volatile, Meathead Movers partnered with a local women's shelter to vet the requests for help to protect the women and the moving crew. The company has now launched an initiative named #MoveToEndDV to inspire businesses to be creative in ways to help victims of domestic violence[73]. Meathead Movers in their Red Goldfish advocates for women affected by domestic violence in their communities not only in a direct and focused way (moving them) but also by raising awareness with other businesses so that they, too, can help.

SUBCATEGORY: COOPERATIVES

Co-ops are advocacy groups where the members are also the recipients of the benefits. This is a club where each person is expected to do their part and all gather together to keep their group strong. There is a real feeling of family within the membership. Membership in these groups implies both a benefit and a responsibility. All members will reap the rewards of the group, but there is an expectation that each must do his part to keep the group strong. Typically, the group bonds working toward common goals, in this case, a shared purpose.

10. REI PURPOSE STATEMENT

To inspire, educate, and outfit for a lifetime of outdoor adventure and stewardship

Backstory: In 1938, Lloyd and Mary Anderson formed the Recreational Equipment Cooperative with the help of lawyer Ed Rombauer. Their plan was to share quality outdoor gear with their fellow climbing buddies. Two years later, REI had 200 members

---

73. http://www.goodnewsnetwork.org/meathead-movers-helps-women-leave-abusive-homes/

and earned $3,000 in annual sales. From then to now, with over five million REI members, REI lives the following Stewardship Priorities:

- Encourage the active conservation of nature

- Inspire the responsible use and enjoyment of the outdoors

- Enhance the natural world and our communities through responsible business practices

- Foster opportunities to increase participation in human-powered outdoor recreation

- Maintain REI as an employer of choice, where employees are highly engaged in the vision of the company and are representative of our communities

REI is privately held and organized as a consumer's coop. REI believes in the importance of building a closer connection with customers through a membership program. REI sells a lifetime membership for $20. Members receive a 10% annual dividend based on their purchases as well as other discounts and special offers[74].

RED GOLDFISH: BLACK FRIDAY CLOSING

REI is embracing #optoutsidecampaign for Black Fridays–and they're paying all their 12,000 employees to take the day off. The goal is building the family feeling that goes with Thanksgiving and carrying it into the next day to enjoy the outdoors rather than be caught in the Black Friday shopping crush[75].

---

74. http://reihistory.com
75. http://www.cnn.com/2015/11/24/living/rei-outdoors-campaign/

REI's Red Goldfish Black Friday Closing gives employees family and leisure time. When other retailers and their employees are in a frenzy, REI is practicing a responsible business practice and contributing to be a worthy employer of choice.

11. BROOKLYN COOPERATIVE PURPOSE STATEMENT

To help those neglected by mainstream banking.

Backstory: Founded in 2001, Brooklyn Cooperative Federal Credit Union is a community credit union operating two full-service branches in Bushwick and Bedford-Stuyvesant in Central Brooklyn. They are a certified community development financial institution serving a population of 300,000 people, 95% of whom are minorities. Area residents have few resources for affordable saving or checking accounts or for mortgages, business loans, or personal loans.

Brooklyn Cooperative Federal Credit Union does offer them those very resources, concentrating on affordability and flexibility of services. It has become a model community development credit union nationwide. With less than $300,000 in their first year, Brooklyn Cooperative now holds almost $25 million in assets and can boast of about 6,000 members[76].

RED GOLDFISH: SIMPLIFIED SAVINGS ACCOUNTS

Brooklyn Cooperative Federal Credit Union offers Simplifies Savings Account to customers who can bring a government issued identification card with a photograph, their social security card, or ITIN card. If those aren't available, a pay stub or health insurance card with their social security number is acceptable. The customer also must bring proof of address. A bill mailed to the home address

---

76. https://www.brooklyn.coop/about/mission-and-history/

will work. They keep the cost low for this service: a one-time $25 nonrefundable membership fee to join the credit union and a $1 per month membership fee. The only other requirement is to maintain a minimum balance of $5 in their savings account at all times. The Red Goldfish for the residents of Central Brooklyn is the value of having a financial institution that considers their financial needs in a way that other institutions fail to do as they fulfill their company purpose of "helping those neglected by mainstream banking."

The next archetype is The Challenger.

CHAPTER 12

THE CHALLENGER

"Purpose is an activating, motivating and animating force. It moves us to get up in the morning, sustains us when times get tough and serves as a guiding star when we stray off course."

— Jeff Klein

The sixth archetype is The Challenger. The purpose of The Challenger is rooted in Maslow's concepts of love and esteem. The goal is to inspire individuals to take individual action.

Type: Love/Esteem

Category: Product to Purpose

Archetype: The Challenger - Inspiring people to transformative action.

Fiction: Maximus

Non-Fiction: General Patton, Phil Knight, Winston Churchill, Tony Robbins, Oprah

The symbol of The Challenger is Maximus from *Gladiator*. Brands with The Challenger archetype seek to become change agents. They want to inspire individuals to become a better version of themselves. In the words of Maximus, "Three weeks from now, I will be harvesting my crops. Imagine where you will be, and it will be so. Hold the line! Stay with me! If you find yourself alone, riding in the green fields with the sun on your face, do not be troubled. For you are in Elysium, and you're already dead! [Cavalry laughs] Brothers, what we do in life... echoes in eternity."

This archetype can be broken down to the following subcategories:

*   General excellence as a goal: Nike

*   Build and empower a community: Lego, Barbie

- Lifestyle: Starbucks

- Build a better system: New Leaf Paper

- Solve a problem: Western Union

Let's look at six brands that have embraced The Challenger archetype. To see more examples of this archetype, visit the Red Goldfish online resource library where you'll find hundreds of great examples, training videos, and more case studies. Go to 602communications.com/redgoldfish

SUBCATEGORY: GENERAL EXCELLENCE AS A GOAL

This subcategory is about general excellence and striving. These companies believe in determination, hard work, and living your dream. That dream could be anything, but the important thing is to be true to one's self and to work as hard as possible to achieve a personal vision.

1. NIKE PURPOSE STATEMENT

To inspire every athlete... and if you have a body, you are an athlete.

Backstory: Nike, previously known as Blue Ribbon Sports, was founded in 1964 by Phil Knight and Bill Bowerman. Phil Knight was a middle distance runner hailing from Portland who trained under track and field coach Bill Bowerman. Bill Bowerman wanted to enhance runner performance and tried to do this without success by improving their running shoes in his free time. In the meantime, Phil Knight completed his MBA at Stanford where he had written a paper suggesting retailers could have shoes made in Japan to compete successfully with well-known German brands. He even imported shoes from Japan himself and tried to sell them, including to his former coach Bill Bowerman. Instead of buying the shoes, Bowerman wanted to be a partner.

They went through years of struggle until 1972 when they began to have some success with a new training shoe they developed in 1971. They launched the Nike Air technology in 1979 and their success continued to grow, leading them to go for Initial Public Offering by the end of 1980. By 1982, they had become the number one supplier for athletic/training shoes in America[77].

RED GOLDFISH: NIKE+ RUNNING APP

Nike+ is not just another fitness app. It has an illustrious pedigree dating way back to the glory days of the Steve Jobs' era of Apple. The iconic orange swoosh app icon first made its appearance on the iPod in 2006 and was presumably approved by Jobs himself.

SUBCATEGORY: BUILD AND EMPOWER A COMMUNITY

These brands seek to bring together a tribe and to be the voice that champions their ascendance. They believe in the cause and they want to stand out front ready to lead an empowered Army to move forward into their greatness. This subcategory has much in common with "the advocate" archetype.

2. LEGO PURPOSE STATEMENT

To inspire and develop the builders of tomorrow.

Backstory: The name 'LEGO' is an abbreviation of the two Danish words "leg godt," meaning "play well." The LEGO Group was

---

77. https://successstory.com/companies/nike-inc

founded in 1932 by Ole Kirk Kristiansen. The company has passed from father to son and is now owned by Kjeld Kirk Kristiansen, a grandchild of the founder. It has come a long way over the past almost 80 years–from a small carpenter's workshop to a modern, global enterprise that is now one of the world's largest manufacturers of toys. The LEGO brick is its most important product having been named "Toy of the Century" twice. LEGO products have undergone extensive development over the years–but the foundation remains the traditional LEGO brick. The brick in its present form was launched in 1958. The interlocking principle with its tubes makes it unique and offers unlimited building possibilities. It's just a matter of getting the imagination going–and letting a wealth of creative ideas emerge through play[78].

RED GOLDFISH: UNICEF PARTNERSHIP

Lego supports children's rights in partnership with UNICEF. The work with UNICEF strengthens child protection governance in the LEGO Group. They were the first in the toy industry to establish a global partnership with UNICEF. They are committed to drive awareness of how corporations can generate positive change for children[79]. The Lego UNICEF partnership is a Red Goldfish for the company as it protects today's customer while it "inspires and develops the builders of tomorrow."

3. BARBIE PURPOSE STATEMENT

To inspire girls, through a doll, to be anything she wanted to be.

Backstory: The precursor to the Barbie doll was not meant for children. Born in Germany in 1952, the inspiration for America's most famous doll was a saucy, high-end call girl named Lilli. First created

78. https://www.lego.com/en-us/aboutus/lego-group/the_lego_history
79. https://www.lego.com/en-us/aboutus/responsibility/our-partnerships

as a comic-strip character in the Hamburg newspaper Bild-Zeitung, the Bild Lilli doll became so popular that she was immortalized in plastic–and sold as an adult novelty, according to Robin Gerber, the author of Barbie and Ruth. "Lilli dolls could be bought in tobacco shops, bars and adult-themed toy stores," Gerber writes. "Men got Lilli dolls as gag gifts at bachelor parties, put them on their car dashboard, dangled them from the rearview mirror, or gave them to girlfriends as a suggestive keepsake." Nonetheless, Lilli dolls were soon coveted by children as well as adults. They caught the eye of 15-year-old Barbara Handler on a 1956 vacation in Switzerland with her mother, Ruth, a co-founder of the Mattel toy company. Ruth Handler brought three of the dolls home with her to California according to *TIME magazine*. Three years later–March 9, 1959– she introduced her own adaptation at the American International Toy Fair in New York. The new doll was named Barbie after Handler's daughter. By the time Barbie turned 50, in 2009, Mattel had sold more than 1 billion copies of the doll, partly by "cultivating its wholesome image," according to *TIME*[80].

RED GOLDFISH: IMAGINE THE POSSIBILITIES

In 2015, Mattel put together a campaign based entirely on the aspirations of young girls. "Imagine the Possibilities" shows five young girls playing out their desired careers in real-life settings, choosing to be a veterinarian, a museum guide, a businesswoman, a college professor and a soccer coach. Each gets to act out her role with the adults around her, who are apparently not pre-warned, playing along while being filmed with hidden cameras. Scenes include a crisp college lecture on brainpower and a rather harsh workout for members of a soccer squad, who are instructed: "Knees up, like a unicorn. Higher, higher[81]!"

80. http://time.com/3731483/barbie-history/
81. https://www.fastcocreate.com/3052116/barbie-tells-girls-they-can-be-anything-and-helps-some-prove-it

SUBCATEGORY: LIFESTYLE

Lifestyle brands extol the virtues of an entire lifestyle that includes all aspects of a person's happiness. Starbucks wants to champion individual expression in every conceivable machination. Their goal is to provide a space where friendships can foster, business plans can be written, downtime can be enjoyed, study can be effective, and a whole variety of community meetings can be accentuated. These brands have a larger vision and a bigger purpose than any individual product feature or single mission. The brand extols general well-being or prosperity through many different paths.

4. STARBUCKS PURPOSE STATEMENT

To inspire and nurture the human spirit one cup at a time.

Backstory: The first Starbucks opened in 1971 as a single store in Seattle's historic Pike Place Market. The Starbucks name was inspired by Moby Dick and brought to mind the sea trade of the early coffee traders. In 1981, Howard Schultz first walked into a Starbucks store. From his first cup of Sumatra, Howard was drawn in by Starbucks and joined the company a year later. In 1983, Howard traveled to Italy and became captivated with Italian coffee bars and the romance of the coffee experience. He had a vision to bring the Italian coffeehouse tradition back to the United States. His vision was for a place for conversation and a sense of community; a third place the fell between work and home[82].

RED GOLDFISH: UPSTANDERS

Starbucks believes stories of ordinary citizens doing extraordinary things too often go unnoticed.

---

[82]. https://www.starbucks.com/about-us/company-information

"Upstanders" is a national campaign to identify and inspire great citizens across the country. The series profiles people doing extraordinary things to help their community or their neighbor.

When asked what he thought was the "common gene" among these "extraordinary" individuals," Schultz described their sense of humanity:

> "We as a country for some reason have lost our sense of humanity, but when we see it, we're drawn to it," Schultz said. "And I think the people that we've met have given us such a gift because everyone has given us the opportunity to see what it means to serve, to be as a servant leader, and I think when you're around these people, you want do more[83]."

Sharing stories about extraordinary people to inspire us all in the Upstanders series is a Red Goldfish for Starbucks to fulfill its purpose of "nurturing the human spirit" even beyond the cup of coffee.

SUBCATEGORY: BUILD A BETTER SYSTEM

These brands champion innovative solutions to thorny problems. Their innovation has revealed a better way, and they attempt to empower an entire community to solve a problem.

5. NEW LEAF PAPER PURPOSE STATEMENT

To inspire a fundamental shift toward sustainability in the paper industry.

---

83. http://www.cbsnews.com/news/starbucks-ceo-howard-schultz-upstanders-first-
original-series-2016-race-hillary-clinton/

Backstory: The paper industry is one of the most polluting and re-source intensive industries in the world. It is responsible for over a third of worldwide timber harvest and over 40% of all landfill waste in the U.S. When New Leaf Paper was founded in 1998, the paper industry had demonstrated a high resistance to change. With low margins, a commoditized international market, and huge capital investment in the status quo, paper companies resisted efforts to integrate sustainable principles into their business practices. New Leaf Paper was founded specifically to change this picture–with the mission of leading a shift toward sustainability in the paper indus-try. The company developed a unique approach to business, em-bedding its social and environmental values into every product line and every business relationship. New Leaf Paper's innovative strat-egy is solving the classic "chicken or the egg" dilemma in the paper industry, in which both the supply side and the demand side of the market were unable to change their behavior.

Leveraging the strength and clarity of the company's mission, New Leaf Paper developed a market for truly environmentally responsi-ble papers and served this market through leading product innova-tion. Since 1998, [they] have led the industry with environmentally responsible papers that compete aesthetically and economically with leading virgin-fiber papers. New Leaf Paper founder Jeff Men-delsohn states: "Let non-profits focus on the issues. Business should focus on the solutions[84]."

RED GOLDFISH: ECOAUDIT

By choosing New Leaf Paper, a company demonstrates its commit-ment to be an environmentally and socially responsible business. The New Leaf Paper EcoAudit helps communicate a business' lead-ership and sustainability and measures its impact on the environ-ment in a way that is transparent and backed by trusted institutions.

---

84. http://newleafpaper.com/our-story/

The EcoAudit shows the tangible environmental benefits—savings in trees, water, energy, solid waste and greenhouse gases—of using post-consumer recycled paper instead of virgin paper. Many customers reproduce the New Leaf EcoAudit in their printed materials to demonstrate their environmental leadership and the positive impact of their paper choices[85]. New Leaf Paper 's EcoAudit helps companies become more aware of their environmental and social responsibilities in their responsible use of paper products and offers sustainable, environmentally friendly solutions for those companies who are ready to take those steps.

SUBCATEGORY: SOLVE A PROBLEM

These brands saw a thorny problem and took it upon themselves to rally the world to solve it. They are doing their part through innovation and hard work. Typically, these brands will discover an injustice or a tribe being oppressed, and they will seek to champion them.

6. WESTERN UNION PURPOSE STATEMENT

To help create a better world through money movement and payment services.

Backstory: In 1851, The New York and Mississippi Valley Printing Telegraph Company, Western Union's predecessor, was formed by a group of businessmen in Rochester, New York. Five years later the company became The Western Union Telegraph Company, signifying the union of "western" telegraph lines with eastern lines into one system, following a series of telegraph system acquisitions. In 1871, Western Union introduced Money Transfer services nationally[86].

---

85. http://newleafpaper.com/ecoaudit/

86. http://www.payment-solutions.com/history.html

RED GOLDFISH: WESTERN UNION STANDS #WITHREFUGEES

Last year, 80% of Western Union employees donated their own money to the WU Foundation to support refugee education and other causes. Employees also took part in volunteering opportunities and business projects in an effort to prevent a potential lost generation through the refugee crisis. Many employees live a long way from the most affected borders, but as global citizens they want to find ways to help[87]. Western Union's Red Goldfish #WithRefugees gives WU employees the chance to help "create a better world" though donating money and time to give refugees a better life.

The next archetype is The Unifier.

---

87. https://www.westernunion.com/blog/refugee/

CHAPTER 13

THE UNIFIER

"Purpose is shared sense of "Why do we exist?" and "What is the essence of how we do things around here?" It was what gave exceptional companies a compass to steer by, and enabled them to adapt and thrive in periods of great economic and social change."

— Binney

The seventh archetype is The Unifier. The purpose of The Unifier is rooted in Maslow's concepts of esteem and self-actualization. The goal is to command individuals to join a movement.

Type: Esteem/Self

Category: Purpose

Archetype: The Unifier - Commanding individuals to join a movement

Fiction: William Wallace

Non-Fiction: Bono, Abraham Lincoln, FDR, Yves Chouinard, Susan B. Anthony

The symbol of The Unifier is Scottish freedom fighter William Wallace from the movie *Braveheart*. Brands with The Unifier archetype seek to lead others. They want to set the future standard. In the words of William Wallace, "Help me.
In the name of Christ, help yourselves. Now is our chance. Now. If we join, we can win. If we win, well then we'll have what none of us has ever had before: a country of our own."

The archetype can be broken down into four subcategories:

- Community builders: Whole Foods

- Revolutionaries: Terracycle, Veritable Vegetable, Revolution Foods

- Uplifters: Fenugreen

- Supporters: prAna

Let's look at six brands that have embraced The Unifier archetype. To see more examples of this archetype, visit the Red Goldfish online resource library where you'll find hundreds of great examples, training videos, and more case studies. Go to 602communications. com/redgoldfish

SUBCATEGORY: COMMUNITY BUILDERS

These businesses actively seek to recruit a tribe of like-minded people to come together and support each other as a community. Typically, the glue that binds the group together is a cause or goal. All of the members believe passionately in the cause. By coming together, they seek to support each other, provide camaraderie, and help guide each other along the path. Most of the time, these communities are local and face-to-face, although they don't need to be. Often times, technology allows these communities to have close relationships despite long distances. The key is that this group seeks a more personal experience with the other members of the group. They are in it not only to achieve a goal but also for the benefits that come from the interaction and support of like-minded people.

1. WHOLE FOODS PURPOSE STATEMENT

To set the standards of excellence for food retailers.

Backstory: In 1978, twenty-five-year-old college dropout John Mackey and twenty-one-year-old Renee Lawson, borrowed $45,000 from family and friends to open the doors of a small natural foods store called SaferWay in Austin, Texas. When the couple got booted out of their apartment for storing food products there, they decided to simply live at the store. Since it was zoned commercial, there was no shower stall. Instead, they bathed in the Hobart dishwasher, which had an attached water hose. Two years later, John and Renee partnered with Craig Weller and Mark Skiles to merge SaferWay with their Clarksville Natural Grocery, resulting in the opening of the original Whole Foods Market on September 20, 1980. At 10,500 square feet and a staff of 19, this store was quite large in comparison to the standard health food store of the time. Less than a year later, on Memorial Day in 1981, the worst flood in 70 years devastated the city of Austin. Caught in the floodwaters, the store's inventory was wiped out and most of the equipment was damaged. The losses were approximately $400,000 and Whole Foods Market had no insurance. Customers and neighbors voluntarily joined the staff to repair and clean up the damage. Creditors, vendors, and investors all provided breathing room for the store to get back on its feet, and it re-opened only 28 days after the flood. Beginning in 1984, Whole Foods Market began its expansion out of Austin, first to Houston and Dallas and then into New Orleans. Today there are 467 stores throughout North America and the United Kingdom[88].

RED GOLDFISH: ORGANIC FOOD STANDARDS

Whole Foods' standards aren't standard anywhere else. Every year there's more demand for "sustainable food" and "natural food products." In developing their standards, they research everything from food additives to antibiotics in meat production, sustainable seafood to organic skin care. If you want quality assurance about what goes into the products you buy, their standards make it easy, because if the product doesn't meet their high standards, they don't sell it. There are many definitions out there for "natural food products" and many opinions on what food additives to avoid. Among other criteria, they draw a line when it comes to hydrogenated fats and

---

artificial colors, flavors, preservatives, and sweeteners. Here are the Whole Foods stated quality standards:

- We carefully evaluate each and every product we sell.

- We feature foods that are free of artificial preservatives, colors, flavors, sweeteners, and hydrogenated fats.

- We are passionate about great tasting food and the pleasure of sharing it with others.

- We are committed to foods that are fresh, wholesome and safe to eat.

- We seek out and promote organically grown foods.

- We provide food and nutritional products that support health and well-being.

SUBCATEGORY: REVOLUTIONARIES

Revolutionaries tend to be focused on bigger causes and less on a specific transgression. These are companies that seek progress on many different fronts for their constituents. They are seeking liberation for their members, not just righting an individual wrong. Terracycle seeks to unite recycling and manufacturing in a new dawn of practical sustainability. They don't just seek to have less waste on the planet. Most of these companies have very big missions that are firmly focused on their customers' lives. This is transcendent change that moves entire classes of people forward.

The key here is that these groups are more of a social change agent than a problem solver. They enjoy stirring the pot. They revel in poking a sharp stick at the established order. They are natural troublemakers and proud of it.

2. TERRACYCLE PURPOSE STATEMENT

To be an international leader in recycling the unrecyclable.

Backstory: Tom Szaky founded TerraCycle in 2001 as a freshman at Princeton University. He and another student fed dining hall leftovers to worms and liquefied the worm compost, creating an organic and highly effective fertilizer. Lacking the money to package their product, the duo used soda bottles they retrieved from recycling bins as containers to peddle the worm poop. "That was the inspirational moment," says Szaky, who decided to drop out of Princeton to pursue TerraCycle as a full-time endeavor. "What got me very excited was ... waste as a business idea." Today, TerraCycle continues to build off the worm compost idea of using other waste materials to craft new products. With eight offices around the world and some 125 employees, TerraCycle runs recycling programs in more than 350,000 locations in 22 countries.

Szaky and his team devise a plan to deal with each type of waste, and then process the waste through refurbishing it into something useful or through reprocessing it for recycling. "Everything around us will become waste," says Szaky. Our focus is on anything that you cannot recycle today, and that is 75 percent of all objects in the world." Szaky grew up in Budapest, Hungary, prior to the fall of communism and has been intrigued by entrepreneurship ever since he arrived in North America. He sees the world of business as a vehicle for positive social change.

"I think business is more powerful than war, and more powerful than politics," he says. "It transcends borders very easily, and it is much more lasting." He rejects the paradigm that businesses are intended only to generate profits and that only charities can do good. His goal is to find a way to overlap those missions. "It requires a really strong focus on purpose, and fundamentally deprioritizing pure profit to a degree," Szaky concedes. While TerraCycle is a for-profit enterprise, its focus on also doing good is seen not only in the millions of dollars it has contributed to various causes but also in the effect it has had on the actions of consumers and corporations regarding waste and its environmental impact. Szaky says that his biggest hope is that more people will be inspired to change their everyday patterns of consumption and reduce the amount of waste they create. "I would love for people to make [TerraCycle] irrelevant through their choices and consumption. Wouldn't that be awesome?" he said. "And then I get to start another company[89]."

RED GOLDFISH: POINTS PROGRAM

One of TerraCycle's initiatives awards points to participants who then can redeem them in the form of charitable donations to schools and other nonprofit organizations. These contributions have surpassed $10 million to date[90].

3. VERITABLE VEGETABLE PURPOSE STATEMENT

To create an alternative and sustainable food system.

Backstory: Veritable Vegetable (VV) became part of a 1970's movement to bring low-cost, nutritious food to neighborhood co-ops and community storefronts in the greater San Francisco area. These collectives, called People's Food System, provided a large-scale alternative to the existing corporate food system. "Food for people, not for profit" was the mantra. Farmers were rekindling interest in organic farming and developing new organic production tech-

89. http://www.csmonitor.com/World/Making-a-difference/2016/0204/Tom-Szaky-started-TerraCycle-to-help-de-junk-the-world
90. https://www.terracycle.com/en-US/about-terracycle/points

niques. VV established relationships with many of these growers struggling with organic production. VV wanted to promote sustainable farming and share information about organic food and agricultural issues. They also began distributing produce beyond the original People's Food System. Through the years, VV has developed certification standards, worked to pass food and agriculture legislation, championed the demand for fresh, organic fruits and vegetables, and helped unify the produce community all the while supplying healthy, fresh foods to communities all over California and beyond[91].

RED GOLDFISH: GREEN FLEET

VV invests in state-of-the-art equipment, uses environment-friendly technologies, runs the lowest emission equipment available, works continuously to reduce fuel consumption, and researches non-petroleum based fuel options, all as ways to decrease their carbon footprint.

Their fleet includes hybrid tractors and refrigeration units run by a mixture of diesel fuel and electric power that produce almost zero emissions[92]. The Veritable Vegetable Red Goldfish, a green fleet to transport their fresh food, is consistent with their purpose "to create an alternative and sustainable food system that values the cost of moving food."

4. REVOLUTION FOODS PURPOSE STATEMENT

To transform school lunches to nutritious food.

Backstory: Kristin Richmond and Kirsten Tobey faced a fundamental design constraint when they launched Revolution Foods on the

---

91. http://www.veritablevegetable.com/our-roots.php
92. http://www.veritablevegetable.com/trucks-and-drivers.php

site of a former McDonald's near Oakland, California. It was $3 for each lunch served. The UC Berkeley Haas Business School graduates were designing a line of healthy, nutritionally balanced meals for California's primary and secondary school students, and had to innovate radically to stay within school systems' tight budgets. The duo created the company with a mission to transform the way America eats by providing access to healthy, affordable meals. They feel that proper nutrition is a cornerstone of providing our youth the nourishment they need to lead successful lives. They did it by saying no. No high fructose corn syrup, no artificial colors, no artificial flavors, or artificial sweeteners. They are on a quest to build lifelong healthy eaters by making kid-inspired, chef-created food accessible to all. In their word, "Because our kids deserve nothing less." Each week, Revolution Foods serves over one and a half million freshly prepared, healthy meals to students across the country[93].

RED GOLDFISH: FEEDING GOOD FUND

Revolution Foods believes in bringing things full circle. One percent of retail sales are donated back to schools through the company's Feeding Good Fund, which provides grants to schools that need equipment to serve freshly prepared meals to their students[94].

SUBCATEGORY: UPLIFTERS

This category has much more of a half full glass feel than the previous two. Typically, these are not organizations that focus on a transgression, but see a glorious positive future for their constituents and actively seek to improve their lives. This group invites others to join them as they advocate and help a group of people move up and onward to a better day. This category is very close to "amass to

---

93. http://revolutionfoods.com/about/
94. http://revolutionfoods.com/in-stores/

cheer for constituency" but in this case there are pragmatic things that can be done in order to uplift their constituents. Typically these organizations have big plans for their members. The companies are busy advocating on their behalf. The tone here is demonstratively positive. It is going to be a new day and a bright future as their participants make steady progress toward their goals.

5. FENUGREEN PURPOSE STATEMENT

To make organic produce fresh for all.

Backstory: Fenugreen was founded by two friends, Kavita M. Shukla and Swaroop Samant. Shukla developed and patented FreshPaper while in high school after she stumbled upon its spices and botanicals in a medicinal hot drink given to her by her grandmother in India to prevent a reaction to contaminated tap water. A shocking 25 percent of the world's food supply is lost to spoilage. The Massachusetts-based company aims to address this waste with its simple innovation. Shukla first began selling FreshPaper at farmers' markets in 2010. FreshPaper, which looks like an ordinary square of paper, extends the life of fresh produce as much as two to four times. It can be reused multiple times before being composted. In 2013, FreshPaper won the INDEX award, the world's largest prize for design, presented by Her Royal Highness the Crown Princess of Denmark. Previous winners include Apple and Tesla[95].

RED GOLDFISH: BUY ONE, GIVE ONE

Fenugreen sells FreshPaper to make it available to those who need it most. They partner with Whole Foods Market because of the opportunity to develop their 'Buy One, Give One' program. For every package sold, Fenugreen will donate a package to food banks

---

95. http://www.sustainablebrands.com/news_and_views/blog/

sbio-winner-fenugreen-poised-change-world-could-your-startup-do-same or nonprofits in less-economically developed countries with the goal to bring FreshPaper to the 1.6 billion people living without refrigeration in the developing world. They also share with food banks and food pantries here at home that struggle to provide fresh, healthy food to the hungry[96].

SUBCATEGORY: SUPPORTERS

These companies have the expressed goal of protecting a group of people or a cause. If the cause or group is to remain robust, it must be protected from bad things. These companies actively advocate for their constituents, showing them that they care about their well-being and they want to do all they can to stand by the members no matter what perils may come.

6. PRANA PURPOSE STATEMENT

To bring greater sustainability to manufacturing

Backstory: Named after the Sanskrit word meaning "vitality and breath," The company was started in a garage in Carlsbad, California back in 1992. At that time, yoga and climbing gear left a lot to be desired, so Beaver and Pam Theodosakis decided to create their own stylish and sustainably made clothes. The company is now a leader in the active apparel sector. It is particularly focused on greater consciousness and sustainability in manufacturing practices. prAna follows the core belief that companies should give much more than they take from the world. Their commitment to sustainability, community, and doing right pushes them to find innovative ways to do good things in a good way.

---

96. http://www.treehugger.com/green-food/simple-sheet-paper-keeps-produce-fresh-4-times-longer.html

RED GOLDFISH: SUSTAINABLE CLOTHING MOVEMENT

prAna believes that organic cotton matters. 84% of the cotton they use is organic. This means farmers and their land are exposed to less pesticides and toxins. They are advocates to help increase demand for more sustainable clothing practices as expressed in their purpose statement.

CHAPTER 14

THE MASTER

*"Purpose is shared sense of "Why do we exist?" and
"What is the essence of how we do things around here?"
It was what gave exceptional companies a compass to
steer by, and enabled them to adapt and thrive in
periods of great economic and social change."*

— Binney

Themes seventh archetype is The Master. The purpose of The Master is rooted in Maslow's concept of self-actualization. The goal is to change lives towards transcendence.

Type: Self-Actualization

Category: Purpose

Archetype: The Master - On a mission to change lives and improve the world

Fiction: Obi-wan Kenobi, Yoda, Gandalf

Non-Fiction: Nelson Mandela, Elon Musk, Bill Gates

The symbol of The Master is Yoda from *Star Wars*. Brands with The Master archetype seek to improve the world. They want to set the future standard. In the words of Yoda, "Always two there are, no more, no less. A master and an apprentice."

The archetype can be broken into the following subcategories:

- Changing lives by building revenue models that pull people up from poverty: Warby Parker, Aravind Eye Hospital, TOMS

- Changing lives through technical innovation: IBM, Gore

- Changing lives through capital investment: Grameen Shakti, Juhidi Kilimo

- Changing lives by connecting suppliers & buyers in more efficient ways: Lyft

- Changing lives through free enterprise philanthropy: Greyston Bakery

- Changing lives by providing healthy alternatives: CVS

Let's look at 10 brands that have embraced The Master archetype. To see more examples of this archetype, visit the Red Goldfish on-line resource library where you'll find hundreds of great examples, training videos, and more case studies. Go to 602communications. com/redgoldfish

SUBCATEGORY: CHANGING LIVES BY BUILDING REVENUE MODELS THAT PULL PEOPLE UP FROM POVERTY

These are brands that have found a way to fund a business that actively helps people improve their lives. Typically, those helped are disadvantaged communities in third-world nations, but they can also include disadvantaged people trying to overcome some difficulty such as a physical handicap, imprisonment, or social disadvantage. These businesses often sell premium products so that they are able to set aside monies for doing good. Their buyers are purchasing not only a product, but they are also doing good at the same time, making the premium purchase a worthy investment for them. The feeling of having helped others is a monetizable asset that organizations can attach to almost any product. The secret is that purpose must be the foundation of the business. Then the products become a tangible talisman of the deeply instinctual need we all have to care for those who have less than we do.

1. WARBY PARKER PURPOSE STATEMENT

To offer designer eyewear at a revolutionary price, while leading the way for socially conscious businesses.

Backstory: Warby Parker is a company that hit its first-year sales target three weeks after the company launched. It began in 2008 with four Wharton MBA students named Neil Blumenthal, Dave

Gilboa, Andy Hunt, and Jeff Raider when they pondered why glasses were so expensive and why glasses weren't sold online. Blumenthal worked at a nonprofit called VisionSpring. VisionSpring trains women in the developing world to give eye exams and sell glasses. Blumenthal emailed his friends in the middle of the night proposing an online eyewear startup. The three were skeptical until feedback inspired the idea of letting customers try on five pairs of frames at home for free before buying any. And the Warby Parker name? That came thanks to Jack Kerouac and two of his journal characters, Warby Pepper and Zagg Parker. The company didn't launch immediately as the founders were busy finishing their MBA's. *GQ* contacted Blumenthal wanting to do a story, but at that time there wasn't a company yet, and the website was unfinished. On February 15, 2010, WarbyParker.com went live. Within 48 hours of *GQ* dubbing the company "the Netflix of eyewear," the site was flooded with orders for $95 glasses. Blumenthal had to temporarily suspended the home try-on program. Customers were placing orders long after inventory had run out because there was no "sold out" function on the website. The wait list was over 20,000-people long. And that was the way the company hit its first-year sales target in three weeks. Today, the company that started with $2,500 in capital has a market valuation of $1.2 billion[97].

RED GOLDFISH: BUY A PAIR, GIVE A PAIR

Rather than donating the glasses outright, the company makes cash donations from its sales to VisionSpring, a non-profit for which Warby Parker founder Neil Blumenthal used to work. Vision-Spring trains low-income men and women to sell glasses in their communities for affordable prices, allowing them to earn a living. This helps ensure Warby Parker's donations actually meet people's needs and don't displace local businesses. As of 2015, Warby Parker

---

97. http://www.inc.com/magazine/201505/graham-winfrey/neil-blumenthal-icons-of-entrepreneurship.html

has distributed more than 1 million pairs of glasses through 10,000 emerging market entrepreneurs. By providing cash donations to create products for sustainable jobs for low-income men and women, Warby Parker's Red Goldfish Buy a Pair, Give a Pair fulfills both parts of the company's purpose: "offer designer eyewear at a revolutionary price, while leading the way for socially conscious businesses."

2. ARAVIND EYE HOSPITALS PURPOSE STATEMENT

To eliminate needless blindness.

Backstory: Aravind Eye Hospitals began in a rented facility with 11 beds in Madurai in 1976. Today, the group founded by Dr. G. Venkataswamy runs hospitals in Theni, Tirunelveli, Coimbatore, and Pondicherry with over 3,500 beds. The hospital group has grown by adopting an assembly line approach to cataract surgery in India. The Aravind system relies on intensive specialization in every part of the workflow to generate efficiencies. A surgeon, for example, typically performs 150 surgeries every week, six times the number common among Western specialists. To further lower costs, Aravind created a sister organization, Aurolab, to manufacture intraocular lenses locally at prices one-fiftieth of US prices. Aurolab also manufactures the sutures and drugs used in surgery as well.

Aravind screens millions of people each year to identify those whose eyesight is threatened by cataracts and performs nearly 2,000,000 surgeries a year. An important part of its business model is multi-tiered pricing or cross-subsidization. Fees from paying patients range from $50 to $330 per operation, including the hospital stay. Aravind performs 65% of its operations free of charge for patients who can't afford to pay. Through its fee income, Aravind is self-supporting and generates enough profit to fund its expansion. With a 30-year record of world-class care, the Aravind model demonstrates that affordable quality healthcare for the lower income population is possible[98].

RED GOLDFISH: LAICO

The Lions Aravind Institute of Community Ophthalmology (LAICO) was established in 1992 with the support of the Lions Club International SightFirst Programme and Seva Sight Programme. It is Asia's first international training facility for blindness prevention. The Institute contributes to improving the quality of eye care services through teaching, training, research, and consultancy. LAICO was founded based on the realization that many of the real issues in eye care are not related to ophthalmology but rather to other issues. LAICO also works to address the under-utilization of existing infrastructure and resources and the lack of good supply chain policies and procedures. It helps organizations develop good program design, effective governance, and efficient management[99]. Laico With Aravind's purpose "to eliminate needless blindness," LAICO is a Red Goldfish to support those striving for blindness prevention.

3. TOMS PURPOSE STATEMENT

To use business to improve lives.

Backstory: In 2006, Blake Mycoskie took some time off from work to travel to Argentina. He was twenty-nine years old and running his fourth entrepreneurial startup. Besides learning the tango, playing polo, and drinking Malbec, the national wine, Blake got used to wearing the national shoe: the alpargata, a soft, casual canvas shoe worn by almost everyone in the country. Blake saw this in-

---

98. http://www.financialexpress.com/archive/-we-set-prices-not-on-our-costs-but-on-who-can-afford-to-pay-how-much-/233536/0/
99. http://www.aravind.org/default/servicescontent/

credibly versatile shoe everywhere: in the cities, on the farms, and in the nightclubs. He wondered briefly if the alpargata would have some market appeal in the United States, but he was taking time off for enjoyment, not work, while he was in Argentina. Before leaving Argentina, Blake met an American woman in a café who was volunteering at a shoe drive. She explained that many kids lacked shoes, even in relatively well-developed countries like Argentina. The lack of shoes made it difficult to attend school or to go to the local well for water. It also exposed the children to a wide range of diseases, blisters, and sores. Her organization collected shoes from donors and gave them to kids in need. The problem was their total reliance on donations meant shoes were not always available or available in the needed size. That meant even if there were shoes, a child could still be shoeless because none of them fit. After traveling with her for a few days and then traveling on his own, Blake begin to think about a solution in the direction of entrepreneurship, not charity. He decided to create a for-profit business to help provide shoes for these children. TOMS was the result[100].

RED GOLDFISH: ONE FOR ONE

TOMS believes in the power to improve people's lives through business. The company was founded on a model that matched every pair of shoes purchased with a new pair of shoes for a child in need. The program is called "One for One®." TOMS has given over 70 million pairs of shoes to children in need. The shoes are always given to children through humanitarian organizations who incorporate shoes into their community development programs. The One for One concept has spread from shoes. TOMS Eyewear was launched in 2011 and has helped restore sight to over 400,000 people in need. TOMS Roasting Co. launched in 2014, has helped provide over 335,000 weeks of safe water in 6 countries. With each

---

100.   https://www.entrepreneur.com/article/220350

purchase of TOMS Roasting Co. Coffee, Giving Partners provide 140 liters of safe water (a one week supply) to a person in need. In 2015, TOMS Bag Collection was founded with the mission to help provide training for skilled birth attendants and to distribute birth kits containing items that help women safely deliver their babies." As of 2016, TOMS has supported safe birth services for over 25,000 mothers[101]. TOMS purpose "to use business to improve lives" is amply carried out by the expanding and very effective One for One program with the buy one, give one philosophy.

SUBCATEGORY: CHANGING LIVES THROUGH TECHNICAL INNOVATION

These are geeks with passion in their hearts. These are the scientists, engineers, and project leaders who are firmly dedicated to a purpose. These companies want to let loose a tribe of goal-setting, big-brained thinkers to solve the biggest technical problems facing the planet. They are passionate about the power of technology to solve difficult problems and to uplift both societies and individuals. They are constantly looking for the next great idea. Through exhaustive development, testing, and re-engineering, they learn from their mistakes and steadily work their way to breakthroughs. These companies make more money and have more innovations because their teams are motivated by a purpose that gives their jobs meaning. They're not just doing the job for a paycheck. At Gore, they're empowering people to get out into nature, no matter the weather. At Autodesk, they're putting powerful tools in the hands of budding entrepreneurs who will create amazing new products.

4. IBM PURPOSE STATEMENT

To "Be Essential" through the concept of "THINK."

---

101.   http://www.toms.com/corporate-responsibility

Backstory: IBM was incorporated into the state of New York on June 16, 1911 as the Computing-Tabulating-Recording Company (C-T-R). In 1914, Thomas J. Watson, Sr, joined the company as general manager. Watson implemented a series of effective business tactics from generous sales incentives to strong customer service. He required the salemen to be well-groomed and professionally dressed in dark-suits, and he instilled company pride and loyalty in every worker.

Employee sports teams, family outings, and a company band kept morale high. Watson had a favorite slogan, "THINK." It became a mantra for C-T-R's employees. Within 11 months of joining C-T-R, Watson became its president. The company focused on providing large-scale, custom-built tabulating solutions for businesses. During Watson's first four years, revenues more than doubled to $9 million. After he expanded the company's operations to Europe, South America, Asia, and Australia and with a decade of growth, the old name of the company was formally changed to the International Business Machines Corporation, on February 14, 1924.[102]

RED GOLDFISH: THINK

Watson began using "THINK" as a means to motivate and inspire the team and in 1935 filed a US trademark for the name. This word is on every room in every IBM building. Employees carry a THINK notebook, and a magazine called THiNK is distributed to employees monthly Every Friday for two hours an online THINK ACADEMY takes place with up to 120,000 people who connect, share and learn[103]. IBM's Red Goldfish is a mission to change the world by connecting and sharing and learning "through the concept of 'THINK'"

102. https://www-03.ibm.com/ibm/history/

103. http://www.brandingbusiness.com/blogs/creating-purpose-driven-brands-insights-from-fedex-ibm-john-deere

5. GORE PURPOSE STATEMENT

To improve lives through advanced materials.

Backstory: On their 23rd wedding anniversary, Bill and Vieve Gore embarked on a new business venture in the basement of their Delaware home. A former DuPont research chemist, Bill set out to pursue new market opportunities for fluorocarbon polymers — especially polytetrafluoroethylene, or PTFE. The company created a breakthrough product called GORE-TEX. The Gore's also introduced novel ideas about how to organize a company and unleash people's creative potential. By collaborating with his fellow associates, the company turned a dream into a global enterprise. Now with more than 10,000 associates worldwide, Gore remains a team of dedicated people collaborating to push our best ideas forward. Those ideas help people around the world, from firefighters to outdoor enthusiasts and commuters to cardiac patients by impacting their lives through a wide-ranging application of advanced materials[104].

RED GOLDFISH: LIFE CYCLE ASSESSMENT

Gore Fabrics has used a tool they call the Life Cycle Assessment (LCA) for more than 20 years. LCA results have shown Gore that the best way to minimize the environmental footprint of a functional outdoor jacket or a pair of hiking boots is to enhance their durability. LCA not only helps them identify approaches that really matter when it comes to reducing their impact, it also provides their partners with an ecological balance sheet that informs their own environmental strategies. Gore Fabrics Red Goldfish LCA tool reinforces the company's ongoing commitment to improve the company's environmental impact through the quality, durability,

---

104.   https://www.gore.com/about/culture

and performance of their products, thus meeting their purpose "to improve lives through advanced materials."

SUBCATEGORY: CHANGING LIVES THROUGH CAPITAL INVESTMENT

These companies believe that when capital is put in the right places, wonderful things can grow. They are dedicated to breaking down the barriers that Wall Street has built. They want to empower a whole new generation of entrepreneurs and businesses to achieve the amazing things that naturally spring from purpose driven companies like themselves. These businesses look for investments with very specific purposes behind them. It might be growing a local community like the Brooklyn Cooperative. It might be empowering a particular group, which is a passion for Grameen Shakti. Or it might be about implementing an entirely new empower technology such as Frogtek's mission to empower small shops in Africa to boost sales and cut losses through mobile phone micropayments. These businesses believe in the power of money to accomplish amazing good in the world, and they want to fund those who believe in a greater vision. They want to put their money to work in ways that match the values they hold dear.

6. GRAMEEN SHAKTI PURPOSE STATEMENT

To bring renewable energy technologies to millions of rural villagers.

Backstory: Grameen Shakti is a renewable energy social enterprise established in 1996 by Mohammed Yunis to promote, develop, and popularize renewable energy technologies in remote, rural areas of Bangladesh. Grameen Shakti has developed into one of the largest and fastest-growing renewable energy companies in the world. Shakti trained its engineers to be "social engineers" who go door-to-door to demonstrate the effectiveness of renewable energy. The company trained local youth as technicians to ensure that people would have efficient and free after-sales service right on their doorstep. Over one million homes are powered by Grameen Shakti in Bangladesh, making the company one of the fastest growing solar energy companies in the world[105].

RED GOLDFISH: VILLAGE TECHNOLOGY CENTERS

In 2005, Shakti set up the first of its village technology centers to produce and repair solar accessories. This allowed production to move from the capital to the villages and solved problems of cost and logistics associated with rapid growth in a highly decentralized company. By 2012, Shakti had installed 45 village centers, all managed by women engineers who, like their male colleagues, live, work, and train in rural communities. Importantly, these technology centers function as incubators for a further innovation: the village energy entrepreneur[106]. Shakti's Village Technology Centers are Red Goldfish that allow the company to deliver on its purpose "to bring renewable energy technologies to millions of rural villagers" in an effective way and, beyond that, to provide livelihoods for villagers.

SUBCATEGORY: CHANGING LIVES BY CONNECTING SUPPLIERS AND BUYERS IN MORE EFFICIENT WAYS

These companies are passionate about connecting people within marketplaces. They are working hard to shake off old inefficient commerce paradigms that add cost and limit access for both buyers and sellers. These companies have created new, more efficient ways to source, distribute, and buy stuff. Many of them use crowdsourcing and sophisticated internet systems to empower these trans-

---

105.   https://en.wikipedia.org/wiki/Grameen_family_of_organizations#Grameen_Shakti

106.   https://www.internationalrivers.org/resources/grameen-shakti-a-vanguard-model-for-rural-clean-energy-7888

actions. The results are new products that could not have existed in the past. Lyft, AirBNB, and Etsy all live within the incredibly complex algorithms and whirring servers these companies build, but the human result is a supplier and buyer coming together for a delightful and rewarding exchange. In the past, these two people could never have found each other. These companies are passionate about their communities and the opportunities that are empowered by the interactions these companies create.

7. LYFT PURPOSE STATEMENT

To reconnect people through transportation and bring communities together.

Backstory: John Zimmer and Logan Green founded Zimride in 2007. The company focused on enabling peer-to-peer ridesharing. In 2012, Zimride launched Lyft to give Uber some competition. With Lyft, Zimride had hooks in short, urban ride sharing to complement its long-distance and campus ride sharing services. A year later, Lyft was giving 30,000 rides a week. The company sold off the Zimride assets to Enterprise in 2013 to focus exclusively on Lyft[107].

RED GOLDFISH: AUTONOMOUS VEHICLE FLEET

Lyft has plans to build an autonomous vehicle fleet. In 2016, Lyft announced a partnership with General Motors to launch an on-demand network. Founder John Zimmer believes that autonomous vehicle fleets will quickly become widespread and will account for the majority of Lyft rides within five years:

We've built our communities entirely around cars. And for the most part, we've built them for cars that aren't even moving. The average vehicle is used only 4% of the time and parked the other 96%.

107.   https://techcrunch.com/2013/09/09/zimmer-green-from-zimride-to-lyft/

Most of us have grown up in cities built around the automobile, but imagine for a minute, what our world could look like if we found a way to take most of these cars off the road. It would be a world with less traffic and less pollution. A world where we need less parking–where streets can be narrowed and sidewalks widened. It's a world where we can construct new housing and small businesses on parking lots across the country–or turn them into green spaces and parks. That's a world built around people, not cars. All of this is possible. In fact, as we continue into our new century, I believe we're on the cusp of nothing short of a transportation revolution—one that will shape the future of our communities. And it is within our collective responsibility to ensure this is done in a way that improves quality of life for everyone[108].

SUBCATEGORY: CHANGING LIVES THROUGH FREE ENTERPRISE PHILANTHROPY

These companies are completely purpose driven. They don't found their businesses with the premise of "how can I start a successful business?" Instead, they start with "how can I further my purpose?" They don't create a product and then search for a purpose to that product. Instead, they start with a purpose and then find the best business model and product that will fulfillment that purpose. What is amazing about these businesses is that founders typically pick products that are a tangible demonstration of the purpose. Terracycle started with the goal of sustainability and went on to create a whole series of products that demonstratively brought life to that commitment. However, this does not need to be the case. Greyston Bakery wanted to help ex-cons and just happened to choose baking as the way to do it. They could've been equally happy picking any other product but baking was the one they chose. Most companies tend to develop product and purpose in tandem, but enterprise phi-

---

lanthropy companies are smart enough to start with a problem or a goal, then find the very best product to facilitate generating revenue, provide employment, or empower other stakeholders in the process. This takes great business skill and, just as in the previous category, these are amazing entrepreneurs who pull this off. Their passion for their purpose is the source of this ingenuity. These are some of the most creative minds in business.

8. GREYSTON BAKERY PURPOSE STATEMENT

To openly hire employees to provide them a better future.

Backstory: Bernie Glassman founded Greyston Bakery in 1982. Glassman recognized that employment is the gateway out of poverty and toward self-sufficiency. When he opened Greyston Bakery, he gave the hard-to-employ a new chance at life. His open-hiring policy offered employment opportunities regardless of education, work history, or past social barriers such as incarceration, homelessness, or drug use. Glassman became a trailblazer and started an Open Hiring movement. He believes there are benefits available to any responsible business with a commitment to its people and community. Over more than three decades of pioneering work, Greyston has overcome the risks associated with Open Hiring, risks that go along with any disruptive and innovative business practice. The benefits of what Greyston has learned can now be enjoyed by other businesses with vastly reduced risk. Benefits include:

- Access to a population of workers keen to have and keep a job

- Powerful brand and customer loyalty

- Advantageous relations with vendors, customers, regulators and community

- Earned media and reduced costs for paid advertising

- Potential reduction in HR costs stemming from having capacity to fill vacancies faster

- Opportunity for local and state tax credits[109]

RED GOLDFISH: CENTER FOR OPEN HIRING

The Center for Open Hiring is a collaborative learning space that evaluates, improves, and defines best practices. The Center facilitates the widespread adoption of Open Hiring and supports innovation in the delivery of community programs for employees and neighbors. The Center is being developed around four program areas:

- Social Innovation Lab

- Greyston Institute

- Open Hiring Association

- Jobs and Skills Accelerator

Initial Center programming includes:

- Specialized invitation-only roundtables for leaders from business, finance, community, policy, and advocacy organizations

- Open Hiring Toolkit for HR managers

- Open Hiring best practices guidelines

Greyston's Red Goldfish, Center for Open Hiring, goes beyond the company's purpose "to openly hire employees to provide them with a better future" by creating best practices around this program and

---

109.   http://greyston.com/join-the-movement/

resources so that other companies can be involved and help even more of the hard-to-employ.

9. JUHUDI KILIMO PURPOSE STATEMENT

To provide loan products to smallholder farmers for productive agricultural assets.

Backstory: Juhudi Kilimo began in 2004 in Kenya as a simple agribusiness initiative within K-Rep Development Agency, a research and development microfinance NGO. By 2009, it had developed into an independent for-profit social enterprise with the mission of providing loans and training to rural smallholder farmers and agribusinesses. 75% of the Kenyan workforce was engaged in rural agriculture and 50% of them do not have access to formal financial services. None of the banks or microfinance institutions help the rural farmers, so Juhudi Kilimo became a profitable business by addressing two major social problems in Kenya–poverty and food insecurity. They try to do good for society and do well financially at the same time. Their ultimate goal is to dramatically transform the livelihoods of farmers across East Africa[110].

RED GOLDFISH: JUHUDI LABS CLEAN ENERGY PROGRAM

In 2013, Juhudi Kilimo decided to create Juhudi Labs to discover, test, and scale new financial and agricultural products, services, and processes. The Labs Clean Energy Program also provides support to companies serving Kenya's rural smallholder farmers. Juhudi Labs currently comprises four programs: the Financial Product Program, the Clean Energy Program, the Startup Residency Program, and the Field Research Program. The underlying assumption

---

110.   https://www.theguardian.com/sustainable-business/tete-a-tete-nat-robinson-ceo-juhidi-kilimo

of the Juhudi Labs programs is that the products and services being tested or developed are relevant and beneficial to smallholder farmers, helping farming businesses grow and creating a positive impact in farmers' lives and communities. The Juhudi Labs Clean Energy Program introduced credit financing for renewable energy products, such as solar lamps and home lighting systems and biogas plants and cookstoves with higher fuel efficiency and lower carbon emissions. The Clean Energy Program began in 2013 as a pilot project in which Juhudi Kilimo teamed up with d.light, a leading solar lamp manufacturer, to supply solar lights to their farmer clients on attractive credit terms, often as supplementary "top-ups" to their main asset loans from Juhudi. The partnership solved key problems for all parties. Juhudi Kilimo was able to offer its farmers a money-saving, environmentally friendly product in addition to its core asset loan. d.light was able to extend its reach and supply into very rural communities with high demand for solar products. And farmers were able to get useful and desirable renewable energy products delivered to their doorsteps with conducive financing terms[111].

The Juhudi Labs broaden the help Juhudi Kilimo describes in its purpose to provide loan products to smallholder farmers for productive agricultural assets by relevant and helpful products in to rural communities that would otherwise lack access to them.

SUBCATEGORY: CHANGING LIVES BY PROVIDING HEALTHY ALTERNATIVES

This subcategory is heavily influenced by the green movement, the organic movement, and the sustainability movement. All three of these focuses are fairly new to the business space and that is why they are so popular. 15 years ago, getting organic *anything* was hard to do. No one was that worried about sustainability when making a

---

111.   http://juhudikilimo.com/juhudi-labs/

product. Most manufacturers relentlessly sought the best features at the lowest price. Times have really changed. Nowadays, most product categories have many different high quality brands available at a good price. Revolutionary manufacturing advances mean that any product that's a hit today can be quickly copied and on the shelf within just a few months. Businesses have hopped on the green bandwagon in droves because it is fairly easy to implement. Generally, it is not hard for anyone producing a product to create that product in a more sustainable way without incurring exorbitant cost. It is a popular thing to do and that is why it is one of the most used purposes in the brands we studied. But now that every business has a green product coming out, it makes it very hard to stand out in this category. Seems these days that everyone, everywhere has some organic or sustainable goal for everything from banking to construction to shampoo. At their heart, these brands are all about fear. Chemicals in your food will hurt you. Your diapers are killing the planet. Your cleaning products are poisoning your family. Most of these brands position themselves as the saviors of the product category, and the mainstream brands as polluters and poisoners out to destroy the planet. They showcase other brands as selfish money-grubbers. The brands we're including in subcategories are the ones who have managed to escape this blame game. Their purpose is typically driven by a desire to get back to nature and live a well-rounded, balanced life. They position themselves as an indulgent self-care product, not an escape from pesticides and poisons. In a stressed out world where abuse to one's self is almost routine, just walking into a Whole Foods store feels like a nurturing cleanse. Just standing next to the organic produce and walking down the aisle of preservative-free, locally sourced, naturally packaged, perfume-free bath products feels like a soothing retreat. These products are often an escape, a free pass that makes all of us feel as though we're going to live an indulgently long life. Master brands that showcase health have a focus on nurturing and optimizing health. They stay away from shaming those who destroy themselves and the planet.

These brands leave us feeling closer to mother nature and proud of the fact that we're taking such good care of ourselves. They have us beaming with pride that we are part of an exclusive club—those who live in harmony with other people and the whole planet.

10. CVS PURPOSE STATEMENT

To help people on their path to better health.

Backstory: Brothers Stanley and Sidney Goldstein and partner Ralph Hoagland opened the first CVS store in 1963 in Lowell, Massachusetts. CVS stands for Consumer Value Stores. The store sold health and beauty products. By 1964, the chain had grown to 17 stores and in its third year, the company began operating stores with a pharmacy department. The company expanded rapidly both through growth and acquisition. In less than 50 years, over 75% of the US population lived within three miles of a store. In 2014, CVS renamed itself CVS Health and became a pharmacy innovation company that is reinventing pharmacy and healthcare[112].

RED GOLDFISH: KICKIN' BUTTS

In 2014, CVS Caremark made a bold move and stopped selling cigarettes and other tobacco products as part of becoming more of a health care provider than a largely retail business. Stores now offer mini clinics and health advice to aid customers visiting its pharmacies. The decision to "kick butts" took away an estimated $2 billion in sales from customers buying cigarettes and other products. "We have about 26,000 pharmacists and nurse practitioners helping patients manage chronic problems like high cholesterol, high blood pressure and heart disease, all of which are linked to smoking," said Larry J. Merlo, chief executive of CVS. "We came to the decision that cigarettes and providing health care just don't go together in

---

112. https://cvshealth.com/about/company-history

the same setting." CVS also created a web resource at cvs.com/quit-smoking. The company received over one million visits to the site in its first year[113]. CVS Health's "Kickin Butts" Red Goldfish move took away an estimated $2 billion in tobacco and related product sales, but the move strongly fulfilled their purpose "to help people on their path to better health."

113.   https://www.nytimes.com/2014/02/06/business/cvs-plans-to-end-sales-of-tobacco-products-by-october.html

PART III

CREATING PURPOSE

CHAPTER 15

DEVELOPING A PURPOSE STATEMENT

"In the culture of Okinawa, ikigai is thought of as a reason to get up in the morning; that is, a reason to enjoy life. It is suggested as one of the reasons people in the area have such long lives."

— Dan Buettner, TEDx Talk

Hopefully, by this point in the book, you've come up with a few ideas on a purpose that might be a good fit for your company. If you're like most people, the task of formulating, developing, and implementing that purpose can seem a bit daunting. You may wonder how you can convince your organization to get on board and develop a business purpose that fits with your company culture, organizational structure, and competitive challenges.

In the course of the average workday, very few staffers will ever mention or ever think about their company's purpose and mission. The day-to-day tasks of driving revenue and keeping the operation humming take up most of our time and mental energy.

Most of us tend to rely on senior managers to articulate the purpose of a business and then to build systems that bring that purpose to life. But managers typically are focused on the logistics of projects in the pipeline rather than whether those projects demonstrate the company's core purpose.

Some companies have clearly articulated their vision within their strategic documents while others never mention vision at all. There are many amazing purpose-driven companies that never sat down and created a purpose definition document. Typically they are blessed with leaders who intrinsically stay on purpose by following their own internal compass.

No question, having a written purpose statement is a huge asset in communicating a purpose, but it's not something you need to worry about in the beginning stages. You can get to that later. Right now, the important thing is that you start and follow that fire in your belly that brings more meaning to your work and the work done by everyone in the company.

GETTING STARTED

The beginning stages are all about formulating and then learning to articulate your vision. Before you can share your thoughts about your company's business purpose, the thoughts should be directed to something tangible and they should be easily understood.

As you begin to formulate, it is important that you carefully consider the beliefs and attitudes of your coworkers. Most businesses tend to follow the tradition business model goals of Milton Friedman. They see their company as principally a **transactional** entity. Business purpose is primarily embodied in the products they make, not in the Zeitgeist of the organization. Most believe that if the business is making money and clients are satisfied, the company is on purpose. They feel that if they take care of the basics, the larger concerns like purpose are not really necessary.

Some will even see purpose discussions as an indulgent dalliance that could be a distraction from the primary goal—making money. Anyone who saunters into the boss's office and demands a purpose statement is probably going to be told to get back to work and refocus their priorities on the tasks at hand.

The best purpose statements are initiated and shepherded by top managers but if your company managers have not articulated their vision does that mean you should browbeat them into it?

When developing an effective purpose statement it is important to remember that the process is one of **evolution** and not **revolution**. In our training and consulting work we often see purpose statements that have been created in a vacuum by a well-meaning committee. Purpose statements created by sequestered groups are sometimes created solely for PR reasons. The purpose statement will appear boldly at the top of the annual report and in other public documents, then be shelved and never seen again.

These purpose statements can contain lofty, unattainable goals that have little to do with reality. Read through many company purpose statements and you'll find laudable goals that are, however, completely detached from the company's day-to-day operations. Purpose statements must embrace real-world conditions. They cannot ignore the pragmatic truths, momentum, phobias, and dysfunctions that are a part of any company. They cannot underestimate the major forces of company culture, financial realities, competitive pressures, and other important marketplace conditions.

Whatever purpose your company creates, it's important that you not delude yourself. Living a strong company purpose is going to be very hard work and will often require very hard choices being made. CVS stopped selling cigarettes because it conflicted with their purpose to help customers live healthier lives. That decision was a frightening one because it meant CVS would be eliminating a very profitable product line. Today, the company is glad it made that call, but at the time, it was hotly debated within the company.

STARTING CONVERSATIONS

The process of developing a company purpose statement should start small. It should begin with casual conversations around the water cooler. It should be an unpretentious, friendly conversation among coworkers. It could begin with an easygoing question to your supervisor.

Questions like, "What is the purpose of our entire organization?" can be somewhat daunting. We recommend that you make the language more approachable and that you focus on the day-to-day priorities of your company. A good question we like to use is "what's the good our company hopes to do for our customers, employees, and community?"

Realize that these conversations will take a bit of persistence. The first response you likely will get to the question above will have a **product-focused** response. "What good do we do?" will solicit a reply such as, "We produce fantastic products at a good price and deliver real value for our customers." While that's true, it's also what every company in the world hopes to do. That's not a description of your purpose, it's a description of your daily operational goals. It's a tactic, not a goal. That response doesn't adequately describe the consequences and outcomes of all that hard work your company does each day.

Be sure to follow up the product-focused response with "why do we do that?" Then keep asking "why" until that person reveals their larger vision of the company's overarching purpose.

A typical conversation might go something like this. Let's say you work for a dry cleaning company.

You: "What's the good our company hopes to do for our customers, employees, and community?"

Coworker: "We want our customers to have clean, fresh clothes."

You: "Why do we do that?"

Coworker: "Because when they feel they look their best, they are more confident at work."

You: "Why do you want them to feel more confident at work?"

Coworker: "Because when they feel more confident, they enjoy their work more and will advance in their career."

You: "What I hear you saying is that the purpose of our company is to help people advance in their careers. Is that our company's purpose?"

What you will notice about this conversation is that we quickly took the conversation from a discussion of daily business tasks to a conversation about *the effects* of those tasks. Keep climbing up, one step at a time. Mirror the person's last response, putting a "why" in front of it. Use this "why" technique until you've gotten to a bigger place that is a description of an important priority that is key to your customer's vision of herself.

You'll know you've arrived when you are no longer talking about what your company manufactures and are discussing something that would really bring a smile to your stakeholder's face. Why? Because these desires are central to your stakeholder's life and would endure even if your product didn't exist.

Examples of a customer desire that a business purpose could serve:

- I want to be a better father.

- I want to advance in my career.

- I want to have more energy to do important things.

- I want to know the people I love are safe.

- I want to stop living paycheck to paycheck.

- I want to find my significant other.

IDENTIFYING YOUR COMPANY'S BENEFIT TO STAKEHOLDERS

The best purposes are pragmatic ones that are not so all-encompassing that they become unattainable. Stay away from "save the world" purposes that lack accountability. For example, turn the inaccessible purpose of "save the environment" to the more attainable purpose of "we help our stakeholders better understand how the products they buy affect the planet." Change the lofty purpose of "empowering local youth" to a practical purpose like, "show parents how to get kids involved in sports at a younger age."

We would encourage you to give a lot of thought to how your company's customers, employees, and vendors feel about themselves *after* they've interacted with your company. What is the effect of your products and services on their lives? How has your company made a difference to them? Again, be sure that you ask that "why" over and over again. If you find yourself describing benefits that are intrinsic to every competitor in the sector, you're probably still mired in the basics.

It's important that you puff up your chest a little and really dig into the transcendent effects your company brings to the world. Sure, for those of us in the daily grind of bringing a product to market, it's easy to lose touch with how that product actually influences lives. People pay you their hard-earned cash to buy that product and that product helps them achieve a goal in their life. If your product wasn't important in their lives, they'd stop buying it.

The best restaurants don't play the small game of just serving food. They see themselves as an important gathering place that builds family bonds. All restaurants are dedicated to a square meal at a good price. A purpose-driven restaurant might be dedicated to making *families stronger*.

Banks don't just loan money; they assure a community has capital to build schools and critical infrastructure to bring jobs to the area. A purpose-focused bank might be a paternal advocate for city growth dedicated to making **great jobs available to struggling families**.

Landscaping businesses don't just cut grass and trim hedges. Well-manicured neighborhoods are less likely to experience crime. A purpose-focused landscaper might be dedicated to **reducing property crime** and giving her customers the **peace of mind** that comes from knowing their families and belongings are safe.

The key is to clearly identify all the **benefits** the stakeholders experience. Sit down and talk to them. Ask them to describe:

- The benefits your products deliver.

- How those benefits make them feel about **themselves**.

- What the specific consequences are of those good feelings and benefits.

- What greater good for themselves, their families and their community come as a result of using your products.

We find that most companies are so single-mindedly focused on day-to-day operations that they rarely stop to consider the greater good they're doing in the long term. It's time your company fully appreciates the power it has and the awesome good things it does. Employees at purpose-focused companies don't just have a job, they have a **daily calling**.

The employees at REI come to work each day to share in the company's purpose to bring the joys of outdoor living to a cubicle-imprisoned nation. The companies who supply Whole Foods Markets don't just restock the bulk food bins, they are helping to teach a nutrient-starved world how to live longer and healthier by eating right.

BEGINNING THE FORMAL INTERNAL ASSESSMENT PROCESS

After you have had a lot of conversations about purpose with your coworkers, it's time to start approaching the managers of the company. Consider recruiting a few fellow employees to join you. Approach the conversation with a spirit of learning more. Just as you did with your coworkers, ask for clarification on how the managers envision the company's purpose. Share your thoughts. Carefully ponder the manager's ideas and look for common ground.

The next step in this process is to work with management to organize formal listening sessions with all the employees in the company. Work with your managers to arrange for small teams to get together and discuss their vision for the company's purpose. Assign each group the task of creating a short written report that outlines *all* the ideas presented in their meeting. Include everything, even the implausible and crazy purposes.

We recommend that the group assignments *not* be organized by department. Try bringing together different team members from different departments. This helps the groups build consensus that reflect the needs of the entire company, not just the requirements of a particular work specialty. This also will help build staff cohesion. When a sales person hears the business purpose ideas of a software engineer, it can be quite enlightening and vice versa.

The benefit of these small group discussions is twofold. We want to hear the best ideas from everyone in the company, but an equally powerful effect is that everyone gets a chance to be heard. If you are to implement your purpose effectively, everyone needs to know they had a hand its formulation. You need the input of the people closest to your customers and suppliers - the frontline employees.

After completing the small group meetings, gather together all of the reports and publish the entire list of possible purposes to everyone in the company. Categorize them by type. Some might be about improving family life. Others might be about helping the environment. Let everyone read every idea. Encourage the staff to talk among themselves and have further discussions.

ASSESSING THE CHALLENGES AND OBSTACLES

Next, it's time to get real about what's actually possible. Assemble the management team and methodically list the economic, cultural, and competitive realities that will influence the choice of purpose.

Start with financial realities. Are budget cuts coming? List that. Is a competitor eroding market share? List that. Is corporate willing to invest specific areas right now? List those. Catalog all your economic hurdles and opportunities.

Next, what will your company culture embrace? Is there an intrinsic sense of purpose shared by your team already? Flesh that out. Is there a bold in-house or corporate leader with a burning passion in her heart? Are there small groups within the company that have already established a departmental purpose? See if that purpose might be a match for the whole company.

While it is important to acknowledge and embrace the positive aspects of your company culture, it is equally important to acknowledge the foibles, dysfunctions and limitations of your team. Are they scared to try new things? Acknowledge that. Is there labor unrest? Own that. Is your team exhausted from fighting off a recent competitive threat? Inventory all of the eccentricities of your team and write those out.

Don't kid yourself here. Too many of the purpose statements we've encountered in our training and consulting work turn out be optimistic dreams with unattainable goals. The successful ones have refreshingly pragmatic goals that are actually attainable. The best plans are ambitious but are careful never to overreach. Don't dwell on negative attributes to the point of pessimism but be very clear on what's plausible and what's not. Better a smaller purpose you accomplish than a lofty one that is quickly discarded.

HONOR YOUR COMPANY CULTURE

We find that the plans that work best are the ones where the company simply focuses and hones what has always existed within the company culture. A lot of people in any business tend to share a similar outlook on their work and its value for shareholders. It is a far easier job to interpret and clarify existing beliefs than to start something new. Once you thoroughly understand the essential foundational beliefs of the team, you can simply uncover what has always existed and continue the journey.

It is often a good idea to look for your purpose within the projects and priorities that continually get the most attention. Seek to attach your company's purpose to the things that already have excitement and momentum within your company.

Where is the buzz and enthusiasm within the walls of your company? Is there a corporate initiative that is well established and well funded? Is there a thorny problem that everyone in the company is excited to undertake? Be sure to pick something with staying power. Remember, if you pick wisely, your purpose can be a guiding force for decades.

NARROWING THE POSSIBILITIES

After the management team has evaluated each purpose proposed by the staff, it's time to report back to the team on the ones that managers feel fit the company best. Give feedback on each of the main purposes the staff suggested. We recommend you use the following format:

- **Purposes that are possibilities**

  Explain why you like them and why you think they are a good fit for the company.

- **Purposes that are not possible**

  Typically, these are purposes that have logistical reasons for rejection. They might be too expensive. They might not mesh with the company's sales strategy. Necessary resources might not be available. Thoroughly explain the reasons behind the rejection of each of these purposes.

- **Purposes that are possible but would be very difficult**

  List the pros and cons of each purpose. Clearly point out what would be required if these purposes were implemented.

- **Purposes that are possible but require more study**

  Lay out the questions that need to be answered. Report on what's being done and when you will report back to the team with additional findings.

GET MORE FEEDBACK FROM THE STAFF

After you have finished your research on the last category in the paragraph above, it's time to get more feedback from the staff. Publish a list of the purpose finalists and get staff feedback from each department. We're looking for honest feedback on how well each purpose would work within the daily operations of each department. Query sales, operations, marketing, and every department in the building. Encourage them to be brutally honest about the viability of each one.

The goal here is to find out if the purposes you've picked can actually be implemented. Are the purpose finalists just an abstract concept? Which ones can actually mesh well with your existing system? How exactly would the purpose show up each day? How would each department change its workflow to make the purpose a reality?

Be very firm with yourself at this stage. Most people in the business world have been through painfully self-indulgent corporate vision exercises in the past. You will most likely encounter some healthy skepticism. Encourage the team to thoroughly vet each purpose. Ask them to explore the practicality of each finalist and come up with a list of how each could mesh with existing company priorities.

After you've assessed the staff feedback, you'll have four possible options:

1. There is consensus on a single finalist.

2. There is strong support for more than one finalist.

3. There is lukewarm support for one or more finalists.

4. There is little support for any of the finalists.

If you're in the first two categories and have found one or more purposes that fit, congratulations! You're ready to move on to the next steps.

If you're in the latter two categories and found little or no support for your list of possible business purposes, you've still got work ahead of you. Many businesses find themselves at this disappointing crossroad. They have put a lot of hard work into listening and a crafting purpose statement. When their ideas are greeted with an indifferent yawn or even condescension, it can be disheartening. However, this isn't a failure. It's a sign that more investigation is required. We find that these are the most common reasons businesses have difficulty finding their purpose:

THE PURPOSES BEING CONSIDERED ARE TOO LOFTY

The best purposes live side by side with the day-to-day operations of the business. Overly altruistic purposes tend to be abstract and need to be re-crafted so they can coexist with the very real problems the team faces each day. Maybe you need to dial back your expectations. Instead of saving the whole planet, start by helping one constituency that is vital in your business's daily operations.

MANAGEMENT NEEDS TO LISTEN HARDER

The workflow of this entire process has been designed to be bottom up, not top down. If all the listening and discussion with the team did not find consensus, it could mean that something got lost in translation when the leaders honed the list of possible purposes.

We find that in some situations, the staff articulates their preferences and the managers simply don't like what they hear. The staff's purpose preferences may be far removed from the business's sales and operations goals. The purpose may directly contrast with the path that leadership has set for the company.

The good news is that we find that common ground can usually be found. It simply requires the management team to roll up their sleeves and get more imaginative on ways that business goals and purpose can get along.

It may also require management to revise its business goals. If the priority business goals directly conflict with the staff's perceived purpose of itself, those goals will not be successful in the long run. Very few people come to work in the morning with a fire in their belly to hit the Wall Street estimates for the upcoming quarter.

The best companies find their business goals by clearly understanding the priorities of the staff and then finding a balance. Smart leaders clearly grasp the motivations behind the hopes and dreams of their team. Those leaders then carefully grow sales and operations goals in the fertile soil of the authentic motivations of the people who work with them.

MORE SERIOUS PROBLEMS NEED TO BE ADDRESSED FIRST

Earlier in the book we discussed Maslow's hierarchy of needs. The premise of Maslow's theory is that basic needs can preclude consideration of higher, more contemplative needs. If you are starving, finding a purpose for your life will probably never enter your mind. The same is true for businesses.

Unfortunately, we sometimes find that when the staff is asked to define the purpose for the business, the discussions quickly regress into a gripe session about everything that's not working on the job. There is always a little of this any time co-workers get together, but if it is pervasive, it is time to take a step back and assess.

Does your business need to take care of more fundamental survival needs that are further down the ladder on Maslow's hierarchy? People who live in constant worry of layoffs or other threats to their basic security are unfortunately in the rudimentary mindset of Maslow's physiological or safety mode. They're worried about simple survival for themselves and their families. Their focus is on paying the rent and putting food on the table.

Any talk of a progressive purpose statement will probably be greeted with inattention, skepticism or both. Their mindset of the entire purpose discussion understandably will be motivated by their own personal survival. Their response is not just an attitude; it's instinctually driven. Discussions of higher concepts like purpose will fall upon deaf ears.

Great, purpose-driven companies often find themselves facing a crisis and must step back to take care of the basic needs of both the business and their team. Our research shows that purpose-driven businesses usually weather a crisis better. Just as with an army that faces adversity, shared commitment is what bonds a team.

Purpose is what gives armies their power. They didn't gather together a bunch of men and women then look for a purpose to stand for. Their nationalistic or moral conviction is the bedrock of an army's very existence. Soldiers can stick together through literal life-threatening challenges because of the strength of this conviction.

If your company is living in survival mode right now and you have not yet formulated a strong purpose, don't try and initiate it when your team is ducking for cover in foxholes. It simply won't work. Fix your immediate problems. Get things stabilized. Then, try again in the future.

We see this a lot in our consulting work. A company will undergo a huge challenge and things begin to fall apart. In order to save itself, the company will seek to redefine its purpose and business practices. While it is wonderful that they're ready to change to a more effective strategy, change management for a team of people running for their lives is rarely effective.

DON'T KID YOURSELF

It is important that you honestly acknowledge the emotional state of your stakeholders. We have had the heartbreaking task of working with businesses that were chomping at the bit to define their purpose, but we had to tell them to go back and fix the basics first. Finding and implementing purpose-driven business strategies is hard for even the healthiest companies. Companies experiencing ongoing crises must find a way to stop the drama. Only then can they implement a purpose-driven brand.

But don't let this stop you from thinking through what your purpose might be. There is lots of hard work that can be done right now, work that can be implemented once the basic problems are fixed. Don't wait until everything is perfect to start. Begin the discussion now as you work through operational problems. Focus your management team. Plan your discussions with staff. Identify your very best features and benefits, then come up with new ways those products could serve all your stakeholders.

IMPLEMENTATION

Once your purpose is defined, it's important that you write it down on paper so that everyone in the company can easily understand it. Great business purpose statements are one or two sentences long and easy understood by everyone. Here are some examples:

Security Company: To empower hard-working Texas families to live safer, more prosperous lives that are free from fear.

Organizational Consultant: To help Coloradans get more accomplished, reduce stress and feel more in control of their daily tasks.

Bank: To help families be ready for tough economic challenges and rise up to live more prosperous lives.

Church: To bring renewed hope into the lives of everyone in our community. We are steadfastly committed to showing how faith can bring peace to any life.

Home Builder: To facilitate families coming together by designing innovative spaces where people can interact and share in entirely new ways.

Manicurist: To be a refuge from the fast-paced demands of modern life. We will bring a new vitality to tired people and help them face the world with enthusiasm and vigor.

Lawyer: To give the people of Topeka a fair shot at competing for a better life. We will be advocates for middle-class Midwesterners in their quest for a level playing field.

What you should notice is that every one of those statements directly addresses what the company will do to empower *the lives of others and their community*. Each one deals *directly* with the change they hope to foster. They're putting a stake in the ground, declaring the transformation they will bring to the world.

A PURPOSE STATEMENT SHOULD NOT DESCRIBE THE BASIC OPERATIONS OF THE COMPANY.

Most business are proud parents and tend to feel their daily business practices are pretty awesome. Their inclination is to make the purpose statement all about *them*, not their *stakeholders*. Here are some bad examples of self-absorbed purpose statements:

We will product the highest quality automotive parts and provide them at a reasonable price so our customers can repair their own vehicles and save money.

We will manufacture ski equipment that is safe, dependable and provides an optimal outdoor experience for people of all ages.

If you find your purpose statement does little more than describe what you do in a day, try fixing it by adding the following addendum to the end of the statement:

"and we do this because we hope to empower our stakeholders to..."

So here is a self-absorbed purpose statement:

"Our sports blog will provide the people of Smithville with all the latest information about local sports teams and the standout athletes in our community."

Notice how this describes the basic operation of most all sports blogs. It does not address the *effects* of that sports blog. So let's add our little addendum to this lackluster statement, then re-write a more powerful purpose statement.

First, the self-absorbed statement:

"Our sports blog will provide the people of Smithville with all the latest information about local sports teams and the standout athletes in our community..."

Now add the addendum:

"...and we do this because we hope to empower our stakeholders to..."

Finally, write a powerful purpose statement:

> "...provide greater financial, community, and scholarship support to local sports teams and local athletes. We want to create more opportunities for kids to participate in sports and get more local kids a sports scholarship."

After going through this little exercise, we can drop the whole self-absorbed beginning. It isn't necessary because their stakeholders want hear how they'll bring beneficial change to customer's lives and the world. They have little concern to know more about how the business operates. The powerful purpose statement at the end is all that is needed.

A PURPOSE STATEMENT SHOULD NOT DESCRIBE THE VALUES OR ETHICS OF THE BUSINESS

Formulating the beliefs that drive a business is a great exercise to undertake prior to writing a purpose statement. Articulating the ethical principles that will be the moral compass of the organization helps create a more grounded purpose.

We find ethical principles are particularly valuable in guiding a business through adversity. Clearly defining the business' ethical boundaries can keep companies from straying into trouble when the temptation to regress is greatest.

Unfortunately, we find that most business ethical documents tend to be more of a public relations tool than an actual operational guide. Typically the ethical bar is set quite low. These documents tend to espouse the baseline values for being a functioning member of society, for example: don't lie, no physical violence, be a team player, respect others, etc.

Wal-Mart has a whopping 11 guiding principles. What employee could recall 11 things, let alone live by them? Here are the first four principles:

1. Always act with integrity.

2. Lead with integrity, and expect others to work with integrity.

3. Follow the law at all times.

4. Be honest and fair.

What you will notice is that this is the same basic "integrity" principle stated four different ways. If a company needs to reiterate an ethical code of conduct that bans only reprehensible behavior, the business probably has much bigger problems. The rule we like to follow is that if the ethical standards listed in the document were taught in kindergarten, that's probably a sign that the code of ethics needs to evolve.

Ethics and values documents have their place, but they are not a replacement for a strong purpose. The problem is that ethics has its foundation in **contemplation**. Purpose statements are grounded in **action** and **change**. Purpose statements are the catalyst of a mission that will move out into the world boldly and transform lives. By all means, companies should define their ethical standards, but ethical documents tend to be reference material, not a guide for metamorphosis. Purpose statements can move you forward. Unfortunately, the professorial nature of ethics documents tend to banish them to the unvisited pages of the company website.

A PURPOSE STATEMENT SHOULD NOT DESCRIBE THE ACTIONS THAT WILL BE TAKEN TO FULFILL THE PURPOSE.

The methodical workflow looks like this: ethical goals > purpose goals > tactical goals. A business purpose must be clearly articulated and properly documented prior to implementation of that purpose.

We find that after working hard on finding a purpose, businesses get very excited about its creation. They are chomping at the bit to get going and show the world the amazing things they hope to accomplish. The temptation is to stuff the purpose statement full of the tactics the company will use to implement its powerful purpose.

These additions make the purpose long and hard to live by. Great purpose statements are short and packed with meaning. They do not delve into "how"; they are firmly focused on "why." Do your best to cut every extra word from your purpose statement and move the plans for implementation and tactics to a subsequent document.

CHAPTER 16

IMPLEMENTING YOUR PURPOSE

"But with lots of good ideas, implementation is the key,
and so we need to keep our eye on the ball as we go forward."

— Mitchell Reiss

Once your purpose statement is written it's time to turn that statement into an action plan. The great news is that there are probably a lot of companies and people who have similar purposes to your own.

You're about to start making some new friends. Typically, we find them to be a fascinating group. Anyone who has the drive and initiative go through the purpose formation process is probably someone pretty special. They are innovators who want to reinvent themselves, their companies and the world in exciting new ways. They are usually very big thinkers with kind hearts.

COMPETITIVE ASSESSMENT

Begin by revisiting the competitive assessment you did earlier in the purpose formation process. Reacquaint yourself with the brand positions and mission statements of your competitors. Hopefully your purpose statement differentiates you from your major competitors, but if you find it's a close match, you'll need to make sure your tactics create a strong separation. Seek to set yourself apart. Resist the temptation to play follow the leader. If you're competitor has done it, you must either do it amazingly better, or choose another way to demonstrate your purpose.

INDUSTRY ASSESSMENT

Next, make your scope wider. Hop on the internet and start searching for other companies in your sector with strong purpose statements. Below are key phrases you might want to use. Combine these words with the names of other businesses or the name of your sector.

• Mission statement

- Purpose statement

- Ethics statement

- Vision statement

- Values statement

- Goal statement

- Corporate social responsibility

- CSR

- Sustainability

- Objectives

Expect to see a lot of mediocrity as you embark on this inventory of other brands in your sector. Most of these statements will be little more than a description of basic business practices and unimplemented dreams of a perfect world. Stick with it. There's some good stuff out there if you do some digging.

GET OUTSIDE YOUR INDUSTRY

Your greatest teachers probably don't reside within the safe confines of your sector; they are out there in completely different professions. The goal here is to shake off conventional thinking and pick the brains of people who share your purpose. You'll be amazed what you find outside your own sandbox. You can then adapt the good ideas so they fit in your business model.

A wonderful attribute of purpose statements is that they tend to cross sector borders splendidly. For example, your business purpose might be to empower mothers to spend more time with their children. There are an amazing number of companies around the world who share this goal. Appleby's takeout wants mom to spend less time cooking and more time with her family. The website el-earningforkids.com wants the kids to get through homework faster. Ford wants to build cars that foster family sharing during the daily commute.

Start by weaning yourself from the need to compulsively track your major competitors. Most managers are intimately familiar with every twist and turn made by their rivals. They can describe every scheme and strategy being implemented. Businesses can often overreact. Staying abreast of competitive trends is a sound basic business strategy, but many take this too far. If a major rival makes a move, there is often a knee-jerk reaction. This gives the staff whiplash and distracts from the primary goals of the company.

Your best ideas on implementing your purpose will probably come from companies unfettered by the confines of the conventional thinking common to your sector. We all spend most of our days inside our own industry-specific walled garden. It's comfortable there, but the steadiness of our routine makes it hard to imagine differently. You might be a local restaurant, but there may be a bank in your community that shares your same purpose. They may have already made some amazing inroads that could be a powerful lesson for you.

Let's say your purpose is to make local communities safer. What other companies share this mission? There is much you could learn about purpose implementation from companies such as Volvo, Schwab Investments, Tylenol, Michelin Tires, Nationwide Insurance, and the Center for Disease Control. All these companies are dedicated to making people feel safe. What was their breakthrough messaging? What's on their social feed? What events and programs have they implemented?

Also, carefully study the customer interactions of these businesses. We find that purpose-driven businesses tend to be more committed to their customers' well being. So many businesses limit their interact with a customer to when she's purchasing the product. They don't really see her as a flesh-and-blood person; they see her as a sale to be made. Their interaction and concern for her begins and ends with her purchase behavior. If she suddenly stops buying, she's dead to the company.

RECRUIT YOUR SHARED-PURPOSE TRIBE

One of the toughest aspects of following the traditional business model is that it can be a tremendously isolating journey. You have the camaraderie of coworkers, but if the company's goal is solely its own prosperity, those outside the business don't usually show a lot of interest. When a company's goals are inwardly obsessed they often will compartmentalize interactions with the world. Those outside the company are classified in one of three categories: competitors, prospects, or distractions. The team hunkers down and prepares to do battle with the forces that will keep them from reaching their internal goals.

If the team's inspiration is solely limited to monthly sales goals or operational benchmarks, it's tough to find the motivation go to work some days. Few people wake up in the morning with a smile on their face dreaming about the joy of achieving this month's benchmarks.

Purpose-driven businesses are different. When a company stands up and declares its authentic purpose to the world, like-minded people and businesses tend to suddenly appear from out of nowhere. They are often hungry for collaboration.

This collaboration is one of the most powerful benefits of declaring a strong company purpose. When the focus of a business expands to include good for a wider group of stakeholders, those stakeholders will often step up, offering up their own unique skills and expertise. When the goal is bigger than just your own bottom line, others take notice. That goal also helps to demonstrate authenticity, which builds trust. And when trust flourishes, cooperation blooms.

Now is the time that you should reach out to other businesses and people who share your purpose. The goal is to create a cross-discipline, cross-industry group who all share a passion for your common purpose. These people will be your support group, your sounding board, and most importantly, your collaborators.

START LOCAL

Are there suppliers, vendors, or other current business partners who might be interested in joining you? Companies that do business with your company often share a similar customer base. If these company partners have not formally declared their business purpose, they might be interested in adopting yours.

Pay particular attention to companies that have similar clientele to your own. For example, if you are a family restaurant, look for other family-oriented businesses. If you are a high-powered investment company, look other companies that serve those customers as well. Examples would include luxury car dealers, churches in affluent communities, retirement communities, real estate companies, golf resorts, recreational vehicle sellers, and travel agencies.

Put the word out through local business associations such as the Chamber of Commerce, the Better Business Bureau, professional associations and cause-related groups within the area. Get in touch with local politicians to ask their advice in finding like-minded business contacts. Politicians are usually amazingly well connected with other businesses in the area and are often willing to provide an introduction.

TAP YOUR TEAM'S CONTACT LIST

Plumb the contact list of your coworkers and colleagues. Put the word out to your team that you are looking for businesses and people who share your purpose.

Reach out on all your social networks. Let the world know your company's purpose then solicit your network to help find other like-minded companies and individuals.

Search specific keywords associated with your purpose and refine your searches geographically. LinkedIn provides great search tools that allow you to do very refined searches by locality, sector, interests, and keywords. If you do not have a pro-level LinkedIn account or have few LinkedIn contacts, search out a more well-connect colleague to do the search for you.

Team up with other colleagues at work to amplify your social exposure through synchronized posting and events. Solicit followers of your purpose to join in utilizing planned social events such as Twitter thunderclaps. A social message with a purpose is powerfully appealing, so be sure you lead boldly with your goal to improve the lives of your stakeholders.

SET UP ONGOING SYSTEMS FOR SHARING

Once you have solicited your network then build systems to make sure you stay connected. Social sharing tools are your best bet. Create purpose-driven groups on LinkedIn and Facebook. This is a place where you can post problems and get help from others in achieving your goals.

Finally, send specific invitations to a select few individuals in the group to form a mastermind group. This is a small group of no more than ten people. Recruit the very best minds, the most capable achievers, and the power brokers. These will be your big-brain advisors who all help one another achieve their shared purpose. Geography should be no obstacle. Seek out the very best people in the world. I am a member of several mastermind groups like this, each with a very specific specialty. Whenever I get stuck, it is these amazingly capable people who are most able to break my logjam.

We recommend that the mastermind group meet using video conferencing services such as Webex, Skype, or Zoom. There is something magical about seeing people face to face and a group this size will be able to have wonderfully personal discussions using video.

SET UP STAKEHOLDER FEEDBACK SYSTEMS

You cannot help your stakeholders without an extensive understanding of their hopes, challenges, and problems. Before you launch into empowering new options for them, you will want to get a lot of feedback from the people who will be on the receiving end of your work. You will eliminate *a lot* of heartache, wasted time, and wasted money if you simply sit down with them and ask them to describe the things about their lives they hope to change.

We usually do this in small groups of fewer than ten people. Buy a few pizzas and gather your stakeholders together for an informal feedback session. Try not to do it at your place of business. Instead, choose more neutral ground like a local library, community hall, coffee shop, or some other place conducive to conversation.

Remember that you are there to talk about **them**, not you. Do not ask them "how do you like my product." Your products probably generate scant attention in their lives. Your stakeholders probably rarely think much about your products.

Their mental attention is dominated by the really important things they hope to achieve in their careers, for their families, and in their personal life. These are the things vital to their happiness and it's your job to understand how these vitally important motivators drive their attitudes and behaviors. Once you understand these motivations, it's your job to mold your product features, operations, and company purpose to serve these important needs.

For example, if you sell laundry detergent, do not just help customers get their kids' clothes clean, help them to be a better parent. If you sell insurance, do not just sell them a policy, empower them to be a strong family protector. Do not just fix irrigations systems, be a neighborhood beautifier.

CHAPTER 17

BUILDING THE ACTION PLAN

"Have a bias toward action - let's see something happen now.
You can break that big plan into small steps
and take the first step right away.

"

— Indira Gandhi

There are limitless ways to implement your purpose and your company will need to find the way that best fits your company culture, competitive situation, and timeline. Here are some things to keep in mind and some characteristics of companies that have been successful.

BUILD AND INTEGRATE YOUR PURPOSE TACTICS

It is easy to get caught up in the altruistic high that comes from planning the good your company wants to do in the world. We find that some companies tend to get swept up in the euphoria. They plan **big** with hopes of having a real impact. It is good to put together a plan with some meat to it, but if that plan detracts from the efficient day-to-day operations of the business, it serves no one.

Your purpose has two very critical jobs to accomplish. It must uplift your stakeholders **AND** it must make lots of money. If your purpose does only the first of these tasks, neither the purpose nor the company will survive. You must build a purpose that pleases both Wall Street and Main Street.

The best way to assure a profitable purpose is to tightly integrate it with the frontline products and business practices that generate the most cash inside your company. Purposes that neglect this have a tendency to quickly become irrelevant because they are not a vital part of the business cash flow. A purpose that is a foundational element of your most important daily operations is one that tends to get implemented.

Use your own best business practices as your anchor and look for ways those workflows can be modified to encompass your purpose. It is exciting to launch a purpose and state your goals, but it is even more important that your purpose settles into a delightfully habitual routine. The best purposes are day in, day out, accomplished in a thousand small ways. Seek methodical integration in every place your company touches a stakeholder.

For example, the sales team at Patagonia is constantly building websites, pitch proposals, and social media posts that discuss sustainability. Their engineering teams are constantly innovating new materials, new supply chains, and new testing procedures that push the boundaries of sustainable manufacturing. Patagonia's purpose of sustainability is not hard to integrate because the company has made it the centerpiece of all their marketing, sales, and operations strategies. From how they take out their trash to how they develop new products to how they compensate their CEO, Patagonia's purpose is the baseline of the entire business plan.

INTEGRATE PURPOSE WITH PRIORITIES

Get incredibly granular on how purpose will show up each day. Follow the internal trail your stakeholders use to interact with your company. Look for small opportunities all along the way. What is said on the phone when potential customers call your business? How does purpose show up on your website on the very first page? How is purpose demonstrated on a service call? How is purpose proven when customers complain?

When your team develops the proposals and builds the products by continually coming back to the words of your purpose, the sheer repetition builds familiarity and makes it a habit. The best purpose driven plans are the ones implemented in hundreds of small ways in hundreds of small places all across the business day.

MAKE MANAGEMENT THE DRIVING FORCE

Too often we have seen companies create amazing purposes that are quickly delegated to committees, HR, or other peripheral groups within the company. Building a purpose-driven company is incredibly hard change. If you hope to keep it alive, someone with real power within the organization must be its champion. Hopefully that will be the entire senior management team.

SET UP ACCOUNTABILITY SYSTEMS

Don't just create a plan "to do better." Give yourself specific landmarks and benchmarks, then set hard dates to get them done. Make sure the programs have the necessary resources and personnel behind them to achieve them.

SHOW YOUR TEAM: NOT ANOTHER DOOMED PLAN

After the plan is launched, plan a major event to demonstrate that the company is serious about making purpose a part its business operations. Remember, most employees have seen a myriad of CSR plans come and go. Too many staffers have learned just to play along and hope that management loses interest. Roll out your plan with some real fanfare and a carefully considered internal communication strategy.

Be sure to follow up with regular progress reports to your team. The most authentic demonstration of your commitment is persistence. Keep the conversation going day after day, month after month. Don't just share the victories; keep your team abreast of the setbacks as well, including what is being done to (overcome/move forward??)

PURPOSE IS MORE THAN MARKETING

Talk is cheap and marketing talk is the cheapest of all. Companies often have a tendency to crank up the purpose-driven marketing messaging, then hope the product lines and operations will catch up later. Mistrust of marketing is endemic. Advertising can point out how a great purpose is implemented, but it can't be a replacement for palpable proof that the company is walking its talk. If you fake it, your stakeholders will call you out, exposing the ugly truth all over social media. Make sure your front-line customer experience provides substantive evidence of your genuine commitment.

AVOID OVERREACHING

It is far better to start with modest, yet attainable goals than it is to create big plans that fail and leave your team disheartened. Plan for a lot of incremental wins. This will eventually lead to exponential success and a steady routine of purpose driven victories. The more your teams see your purpose in action, the more they will know you're serious.

AVOID UNDER REACHING

After doing all the hard work of finding your purpose and creating a plan, the temptation is to let your hair down a bit and relax after the plan has been written. Starting is always the toughest part so you need to make sure you kick this thing off right. Clearly lay out your expectations on new ways of doing business. Plan regular check-ins and progress reports.

SHARE YOUR NEW BENCHMARKS WITH STAKEHOLDERS

If you really want to assure steady progress on your purpose-driven path, then blow up the bridges behind you. Create a system has that does not allow retreat and backtracking. The best way to accomplish this is to very *publicly* declare your mission and the goals you will achieve. Throw it out to the whole world. Give them dates it will be done. Give them landmarks you will reach. The threat of a very public humiliation will keep you and your entire team on track to get it done.

RECRUIT AN ADVISORY GROUP

Gather together a group of your most capable purpose-driven leaders from outside the company. Task them with two jobs: first, to advise you on the best ways to move forward. Second, to provide continual feedback on the effectiveness of your purpose-driven implementation. Outside people not invested in the internal politics of your company will provide invaluable feedback on where you are excelling and where you need work.

MAKING PURPOSE PART OF YOUR DAILY WORKFLOW

Identifying and implementing a powerful business purpose isn't just a professional endeavor; it often spills over into our personal lives as well. After working this hard to identify a transcendent company mission, it's only natural to start asking questions about how purpose plays a role in our individual lives.

The path of purpose-driven business leadership is an arduous one, but I am continually inspired and amazed that so many people turn this professional journey into a catalyst for deep changes in other parts of their life.

It's only natural to seek meaning in our careers. Most of us feel our job is one of the most powerful shapers of our destiny. The majority of people I have worked with in my career enthusiastically do more than is required on the job. They are often most enrolled in their lives when a job challenges them to rise up and tackle an important business obstacle. Most of them put their very hearts and souls into their jobs. They feel deep affection, even love, for many of their coworkers. They beam with pride when their team rallies to achieve a difficult goal.

Our careers shape our destiny in so many ways. All of us have many roles in life: parent, brother, mentor, friend. But when asked "what do you do?", most of us reflexively describe our professional life. Many of us have left high-paying but soulless jobs in exchange for lower paying, more meaningful work. Today's leaner economic times mean a lot of us spend more time with our coworkers than with our families.

Fully embracing a business purpose brings an entirely new story-line to our own very personal daily toil. This purpose is inherent in some professions. Nurses can go to work each day knowing they are saving lives. Teachers know they are molding the destiny of the next generation. Architects build spaces that shape how communities grow.

But most of us work in jobs where the bigger purpose can be more difficult to see. On that cold morning after a long weekend, it's hard to identify how answering those 50 neglected emails can help make the world a better place. It's difficult to find meaning in yet another conference call with the regional manager.

It's easy to fixate on the drudgery inherent in any job. The escape from this self-destructive loop is continually reconnecting with your business purpose. When times are most frustrating, this simple practice can shift your entire mindset. But it requires an unceasing discipline to climb out of the daily-grind attitude. You must recognize and fully appreciate the difference your business makes in the lives of stakeholders.

That bank teller is not just counting money in his change drawer, he's part of a team that's helping local families afford college for their kids. He can perceive that next person in the bank line as just another faceless soul who needs a check cashed, or he can see that person as another parent he's empowering to achieve a family mission.

A truck sales person can visualize herself pounding out her monthly sales quota, or she can visualize herself empowering the transportation needs of an entire community. Because of her, small businesses will thrive. Backyard decks will be built. Amazing escapes into the wilderness will be treasured. Wonderful treasures will be delivered to every corner of her community.

Maintaining this larger view is often easier in our personal lives. We feel good when we sacrifice to help a friend. We perceive driving our kids to soccer practice as more fun than driving to work. It feels pretty nice to slide the envelope into the church collection plate. Why? Because we get an opportunity to reconnect with a bigger, more meaningful mission.

We perceive the lack of a raise at work as a major injustice yet we gladly put up with less money to spend on lunch to pay for an expensive prom dress for our daughter. The net effect is the same. Both scenarios leave us with less money. The difference is we resent losing money when we are out of touch with the purpose of our work. Lack of a raise will seem a lot more endurable when we have the confidence that our work is empowering others.

It is vitally important that you fully step into the wisdom that your job is doing powerful good in the world every day. Your task is to do a better job of **noticing that good**. If you want to feel more fulfilled in your career and enjoy your workday more, make your company's business purpose the centerpiece of your own daily work routine. Build reminders into your day. Put it at the top of your to-do list. Put the words in a frame on the wall. Put it on a Post It in your car. Say an affirmation every time you walk through the front door.

Redefine your own personal job title. When people ask you what you do, don't describe your position, describe your business purpose. Your work colleagues may call you an accountant, but you know you are really a grower of small businesses. Don't call yourself a kindergarten teacher, call yourself a nurturer of childhood imaginations.

Be a catalyst to enroll others in your company. Bring it up in meetings. Mention it at the water cooler. Celebrate when your purpose pays off with your stakeholders. The more you **personally** spread the word, the better you (will?) feel about why you come to work. Be a purpose evangelist.

The most powerful force in the world is not government, religion or culture, it's business. If you want to leave a powerful legacy in this life, begin by changing the way you do business.

CHAPTER 18

THE R.U.L.E.S.

"Constancy to purpose is the secret of success."

— Benjamin Disraeli

There are R.U.L.E.S. to be mindful of when bringing your purpose to life. Here are 10 questions to ask as you create your Red Goldfish:

R - RESONATE

- Will this connect with both employees and customers?

- Is it something that is meaningful to the purpose of your brand?

U - UNIQUE

- Will this stand out in the marketplace?

- Can you avoid being seen as "me to" or generic?

L - LEGITIMATE

- Is the Red Goldfish making a sufficient impact?

- Will it be seen as authentic when connected to the purpose of your brand?

E - EMOTIONAL

- Will this make an emotional connection with your stakeholders?

- Does it strike an emotional chord and will people care about your effort?

S - STICKY

- Will it be remark-able enough to get people talking?

- Is it easily shareable?

CHAPTER 19

FIVE TOP TAKEAWAYS

"Advice is like a tablet of aspirin.
It tends to only work if you take it."

— David Murphy

Here are the top five takeaways from Red Goldfish:

1. THE POWER OF AND

This is not a decision of OR. You don't need to choose profit OR purpose. You can opt for both through the power of AND by becoming a for-purpose business.

2. A NEW BULLSEYE

The new view of business places purpose first. It sits at the center of the business and informs every decision going forward.

3. THE BLURRING OF LINES

No longer will corporate filing status determine a business. The new mold is hybrid. Going forward, you will either be seen as for-purpose or not-for-purpose.

4. RISING EXPECTATIONS

Consumers and employees want to connect with a purpose beyond profit. The new expectation is that business can be a force for good.

5. BIG DOORS SWING ON LITTLE HINGES

Big ideas like purpose need to lived everyday. Beyond words, it's the little things that bring the purpose to life. These Red Goldfish are the straws that stir the drink.

ABOUT THE AUTHORS

STAN PHELPS

Stan Phelps is a best-selling author, keynote speaker and workshop facilitator. He believes that today's organizations must focus on meaningful differentiation to win the hearts of both employees and customers.

He is the Founder of PurpleGoldfish.com. Purple Goldfish is a think tank of customer experience and employee engagement experts that offers keynotes and workshops. The group helps organizations connect with the hearts and minds of customers/employees.

Prior to PurpleGoldfish.com, Stan had a 20-year career in marketing including leadership positions at IMG, adidas, PGA Exhibitions, and Synergy. At Synergy, he worked on award-winning experiential programs for top brands such as KFC, Wachovia, NASCAR, Starbucks, and M&M's.

Stan is the author of six books, a TEDx speaker, a Forbes contributor, and an IBM Futurist. His writing is syndicated on top sites such as Customer Think and Business2Community. He has spoken at over 200 events in the US, Canada, UK, France, Sweden, The Netherlands, Russia, Peru, Israel, Spain, Bahrain, and Australia.

Stan received a BS in Marketing and Human Resources from Marist College, a JD/MBA from Villanova University, and a certificate for Achieving Breakthrough Service from Harvard Business School. He is a Certified Net Promoter Associate and has taught as an adjunct professor at NYU, Rutgers University, and Manhattanville College. Stan lives in Cary, NC with his wife Jennifer and two boys Thomas & James.

Stan is reachable at stan@purplegoldfish.com or call: +1.919.360.4702.

GRAEME NEWELL

Graeme Newell is President of 602 Communications, a marketing research and consulting firm that specializes in emotional connection. Graeme and his team of emotional attachment experts show companies how to change complacent customers into passionate groupies.

Graeme has delivered more than 400 speeches at events in 25 countries around the world. He is known as the example king. His presentations are loaded with cutting-edge techniques used by the world's most passionate brands. He has compiled an extensive emotional connection video library with more than 50,000 examples. He uses this library to teach leaders how to build deep lasting friendships with their customers.

Graeme Newell has done speaking, research and consulting for corporations across the globe, including: GE, Disney, Sony, CBS, Madison Square Garden, Comcast, and Universal Studios.

Graeme lives in Portland, Oregon with his wife Annette.

Graeme can be reached at gnewell@602communications.com or call: +1.919.217.4438.

ADDITIONAL INSPIRATION AND FURTHER READING

Conscious Capitalism by John Mackey and Raj Sisodio

Heed Your Call by David Howitt

Selling With Noble Purpose by Lisa Earle McLeod

Firms of Endearment by Raj Sisodio

The Human Brand by Chris Malone and Susan T. Fiske

Start With Why by Simon Sinek

Corporate Culture & Performance by John Kotter and James Heskett

Drive: The Surprising Truth About What Motivates Us by Dan Pink

Purpose Economy by Aaron Hurst

The Story of Purpose by Joey Reiman

Do Purpose: Why Brands With A Purpose Do Better and Matter More by David Hieatt

Work On Purpose by Lara Galinsky and Kelly Nuxoll

The Purpose Effect: Building Meaning in Yourself, Your Role and Your Organization by Dan Pontefract

It's Not What You Sell, It's What You Stand For: Why Every Extraordinary Business Is Driven by Purpose by Roy M. Spence Jr.

Purpose: The Starting Point of Great Companies by Nikos Mourkogiannis

Leading with Noble Purpose: How to Create a Tribe of True Believers by Lisa Earle McLeod

Delivering Happiness: A Path to Profits, Passion, and Purpose by Tony Hsieh

People Over Profit: Break the System, Live with Purpose, Be More Successful by Dale Partridge

Peak - How Great Companies Get Their Mojo From Maslow by Chip Conley

OTHER BOOKS IN THE GOLDFISH SERIES ON CUSTOMER EXPERIENCE AND EMPLOYEE ENGAGEMENT

What's Your Purple Goldfish – 12 Ways to Win Customers and Influence Word of Mouth by Stan Phelps. The book is based on the Purple Goldfish Project, a crowdsourcing effort that collected over 1,001 examples of signature added value. The book draws inspiration from the concept of lagniappe. It provides 12 practical strategies for winning the hearts of customers and influencing positive word of mouth.

What's Your Purple Goldfish Service Edition - The 12 Ways Hotels, Restaurants, and Airlines Win the Right Customers by Stan Phelps and Brooks Briz. Packed with over 100 examples, the book focuses on 12 ways to do the "little extras" to improve the customer experience for restaurants, hotels, and airlines. The end result is increased sales, happier customers, and positive word of mouth.

What's Your Green Goldfish – Beyond Dollars: 15 Ways to Drive Employee Engagement and Reinforce Culture by Stan Phelps. The Green Goldfish examines the importance of employee engagement in today's workplace. The book showcases 15 ways to increase employee engagement, offering signature ways beyond compensation to reinforce the culture of an organization.

What's Your Golden Goldfish – The Vital Few: All Customers and Employees Are Not Created Equal by Stan Phelps. The Golden Goldfish examines the importance of the top 20 percent of your customers and employees. The book showcases nine ways to drive loyalty and retention with these two critical groups.

Blue Goldfish - Using Technology, Data, and Analytics to Drive Both Profits and Prophets by Stan Phelps and Evan Carroll. A Blue Goldfish is any time a business leverages technology, data, and analytics to do a "little something extra" to improve the experience for the customer. The book is based on a collection of over 300 case studies, examining the three R's: Relationship, Responsiveness, and Readiness. Blue Goldfish also uncovers eight different ways to turn insights into action.

Made in the USA
Coppell, TX
05 June 2021

56913610R00140